LITERARY/CULTURAL THEORY

MIKHAIL BAKHTIN

Literary/Cultural Theory provides concise and lucid introductions to a range of key concepts and theorists in contemporary literary and cultural theory. Original and contemporary in presentation, and eschewing jargon, each book in the series presents students of humanities and social sciences exhaustive overviews of theories and theorists, while also introducing them to the mechanics of reading literary/cultural texts using critical tools. Each book also carries glossaries of key terms and ideas, and pointers for further reading and research. Written by scholar-teachers who have taught critical theory for years, and vetted by some of the foremost experts in the field, the series Literary/Cultural Theory is indispensable to students and teachers.

Also in the series

Psychoanalytic Theory and Criticism
Feminisms
Jacques Lacan
Dalit Literature and Criticism
Ecocriticism
Postcolonialism Now
Marxist Literary and Cultural Theory
Postsecular Theory
Nations and Nationalisms
Periyar
Popular Culture
Queer Studies
Frantz Fanon
Edward Said
Deconstruction and Poststructuralism

LITERARY/CULTURAL THEORY

MIKHAIL BAKHTIN

A CRITICAL INTRODUCTION

E. V. RAMAKRISHNAN

Orient BlackSwan

MIKHAIL BAKHTIN: A CRITICAL INTRODUCTION

ORIENT BLACKSWAN PRIVATE LIMITED

Registered Office
3-6-752 Himayatnagar, Hyderabad 500 029, Telangana, India
Email: centraloffice@orientblackswan.com

Other Offices
Bengaluru, Chennai, Guwahati, Hyderabad, Kolkata, Mumbai, New Delhi, Noida, Patna, Visakhapatnam

First published 2023

034107

ISBN 978 93 5442 156 3

Typeset in Aldine 401 BT 10.5/13 *by*
Akhil Offset Printers
Hyderabad 500 020

Printed at
Navya Printers, Hyderabad 500 013

Published by
Orient Blackswan Private Limited
3-6-752, Himayatnagar, Hyderabad 500 029, Telangana, India
Email: info@orientblackswan.com

Contents

Preface

It was in the library of the Centre for Social Studies, Surat, that I chanced upon Tzvetan Todorov's book, *Mikhail Bakhtin: The Dialogical Principle*, sometime in the year 1988. I had not heard of Bakhtin before encountering this book, though I had some introduction to 'theory' which was gaining prominence in academic circles. In the ten-day theory workshop conducted by the British Council at the University of Bombay that year, I listened to Robert Young, Antony Easthope, R. B. Patankar, G. P. Pradhan and several other academics and critics, but none mentioned Bakhtin. Todorov's introduction in six chapters presented Bakhtin's ideas on language and literature comprehensively. What struck me as original was an alternative approach to the study of language, and a new model of interdisciplinary thinking on concepts such as the text, author, reception, intertextuality and popular culture. As I began to read Bakhtin more systematically, I found him useful in the classroom, in understanding society, and for making sense of the relations between art and society. I remember using Bakhtin's ideas of the carnival and popular culture while teaching texts as diverse as Maya Angelou's *I Know Why the Caged Bird Sings* and Shakespeare's *Henry IV, Part 1.*

In the early 1990s, I published a couple of articles on Bakhtin's dialogism in Malayalam. I remember looking for an equivalent word for 'polyphony' in Malayalam, while writing on O. V. Vijayan's *The Legends of Khasak*. '*Bahuswarata*', the word I finally used, has now become part of the cultural criticism in Malayalam. It goes to prove the extent to which Bakhtin has become relevant to the sociocultural situation in India now. I have extensively used his ideas in my critical writings in Malayalam, particularly in my book, *Malayala novelinte deshakaalangal* (2017), a study on the evolution of the Malayalam novel.

While I was serving as Professor and Dean of the School of Language, Literature and Culture Studies at Central University of Gujarat, our centre for Comparative Literature and Translation Studies collaborated with the Forum for Contemporary Theory in Baroda, to organise an international conference on the subject 'Bakhtin in India: Exploring the Dialogic Potential in Self, Culture and History', in August 2013. Many eminent Bakhtin scholars, such as Craig Brandist and Lakshmi Bandlamudi presented papers at the conference. Subsequently, Lakshmi and I edited a volume based on the seminar, titled *Bakhtinian Explorations of Indian Culture: Pluralism, Dogma and Dialogue through History* (2018).

Over the years, Bakhtin's books have become increasingly available in India. His name is familiar but his ideas are not widely known in academic circles, particularly among postgraduate and research students. I have delivered lectures at several universities and found that he hardly figures in their syllabus or classroom teaching. Even before the offer to write an introductory volume on Bakhtin was made by Orient BlackSwan, I had felt the need to work on a monograph on his concepts.

As the critical literature on Bakhtin has steadily grown, it has become obvious that he has much to contribute to the interdisciplinary courses in humanities and social sciences. Apart from Bakhtin's fundamental insights into the nature of language and dialogic imagination, answerability and artistic process, carnival and popular culture, he has helped us redefine the relation between aesthetics and ethics. The coinage 'poethics' sums up what Bakhtin's system of thought is all about.

My interest in Bakhtin has helped me grasp the dynamics of culture in the Indian context. He was one of the thinkers I frequently turned to for solace and sanity, during the dark days of the communal conflagrations in Gujarat. Bakhtin had suffered greatly in one of the worst purges of intellectuals in history. The concerns for freedom and justice animate his critical writings on philosophy and literature. In the present day, these ideas have assumed greater urgency and immediacy.

In preparing this volume, I am indebted to all the critics who have written on Bakhtin. In the last three years, I frequently found myself living in places where I had no access to my library, because of the Covid-19 pandemic and the consequent lockdown. I gained first-hand knowledge of how Bakhtin must have gone about his work in the most trying circumstances, with no access to the outer intellectual resources.

A steady stream of scholarly works has appeared on Bakhtin in the last two decades. Brandist's *The Bakhtin Circle: Philosophy, Culture and Politics* (2002), Graham Pechey's *Mikhail Bakhtin: The Word in the World* (2007), Alastair Renfrew's *Towards a New Material Aesthetics: Bakhtin, Genre and the Fates of Literary Theory* (2006) are among these works. As I was in the process of finalising my book, I happened to read Ken Hirschkop's *The Cambridge Introduction to Mikhail Bakhtin* (2021). It helped me update the book with more information. I cannot claim any originality for the analysis of Bakhtin's ideas presented here as they have been under discussion for over half a century. I have aimed at clarity, keeping the Indian researcher and student in mind. For students of humanities, Bakhtin will remain an indispensable source of ideas and insights for years to come. It is hoped that the present volume will serve as an introduction to his life and works for those engaged in academic teaching and research in the humanities and social sciences.

I would like to thank the editorial team at Orient BlackSwan: Sreenath S. for taking the project forward despite unforeseen delays, and Ishita Chatterji for her meticulous editing of the manuscript.

E. V. Ramakrishnan
Payyanur, Kerala
January 2023

Chapter One

Mikhail Bakhtin: An Introduction

Bakhtin's significance as a thinker for the humanities cannot be overemphasised. A major feature of his works is the acute ethical perspective that locates literature at the intersection of various disciplines such as philosophy, sociology and political science. He has given us a new sense of how 'intertextuality' operates in literature. Though his major theoretical insights are worked out with reference to the novel, his ideas are equally applicable to other genres of literature. He does not deny the individual as an essential dimension of the literary, even as he focuses on the collective in the constitution of the domain of literature. Some of his major ideas such as dialogism, the dialogic imagination, heteroglossia, carnival, chronotope and answerability have opened up several possibilities in the contemporary study of literature. In an age of high theory, Bakhtin's insightful interventions have taken us back to literary texts and their basic function in shaping the ethical foundation of literature.

Mikhail Mikhailovich Bakhtin was born on 16 November 1895, in Orel, a city situated to the south of Moscow. He was the second of five siblings. His mother and three sisters lived in Leningrad during the Second World War. They died of hunger in January 1942 (Hirschkop 26). He was close with his elder brother, Nikolai Bakhtin, who went into exile early, first living in Germany and later in England. He obtained a doctorate from Cambridge, UK, in 1932 and taught at Southampton University and later at Birmingham University. The brothers shared a deep interest in linguistics and philosophy, and had a strong grounding in German language and philosophy from an early age. They were driven by their passion for ideas and concepts. While Nikolai Bakhtin was full of exciting ideas and grandiose projects, he seems to have achieved very little when he passed away in 1950. The brothers never met after they parted in the chaotic days of the Bolshevik Revolution.

The period after the Bolshevik Revolution was one of struggle and hand-to-mouth existence. Bakhtin spent several years in provincial towns like Nevel and Vitebsk, teaching in schools and institutes of education, while leading an active intellectual life in the company of like-minded scholars such as Valentin Voloshinov, Boris Zubakin, Pavel Medvedev and Matvei Kagan. He delivered public lectures and also participated in debates. He met his future wife, Elena Bersh-Okolovich, in Vitebsk, at a time when his failing health needed attention and care. He was to suffer from lifelong maladies which would severely cripple him. This, however, did not affect his output, as he was constantly working on long tracts and treatises, not all of which were completed during this phase. Bakhtin was not enthusiastic about communist ideology, though he had used the Marxist philosophical framework in works like *Marxism and the Philosophy of Language*, which was published under the name of Voloshinov in 1973.

When he moved to Leningrad in 1924, he was granted a small pension due to his medical condition. Many of his friends like Medvedev and Voloshinov were already there at the time, and he could carry on discussions within the Bakhtin Circle. Despite his status as a pre-eminent scholar of the times, Bakhtin was not known outside a small circle during this time. Clark and Holquist comment, 'Until the late 1920s, Bakhtin was almost unknown in most Leningrad intellectual circles. He had no institutional affiliations, was obliged to publish under others' names, and was valued only by a small group of devoted friends and a few students' (97).

His struggle for survival sapped him of all energy, as the meagre pension was progressively reduced by the medical board. Some of the prominent intellectuals of Leningrad such as Ivan Sollertinsky and Maria Yudina stood by him in the worst of times that followed.

Bakhtin was a believer since his childhood. He was religious, though he did not attend church regularly. His interest in religion was more a result of his philosophical disposition. It was not unusual for people to be rationalists as well as believers. One of his contemporaries in Leningrad, Father Pavel Florensky, was a prominent physicist, inventor and mathematician, as well as a theologian of repute. He occupied important positions in the new dispensation's institutions. Religious beliefs were not outlawed by the communist government. However, by 1928, Stalin had tightened his grip over the ruling party and this resulted in the repression of dissent, particularly in matters of Marxist ideology. Religious activities were suspect and organisations like the Brotherhood of Saint Seraphim were under watch. Though Bakhtin was not a member of any such organisation, his religious views were well known, and this worked against him. He was arrested in December 1928, on suspicion of being associated with a religious group called 'Resurrection'. His medical condition of osteomyelitis came to his rescue as this made it difficult to sentence him to rigorous imprisonment. Many of his friends like Yudina worked tirelessly for his release. Maxim Gorky and Aleksey Tolstoy appealed to higher authorities for his immediate release. He was ultimately sentenced to six years of exile in the town of Kustanai in Kazakhstan.

In the decades following the First World War, Bakhtin devoted himself to philosophical questions related to art and experience. He was strongly influenced by neo-Kantian ideas during this phase. In the second half of the 1920s, Bakhtin explored Freudianism, Marxism and issues related to formalism and linguistics. It was in the 1930s that he took up the study of the novel seriously, working towards a historical poetics of the genre through the study of Dostoevsky's works. Subsequently, he examined the cultural history of Europe to formulate a theory of the origin of the novel through the study of carnival forms and their manifestations in literature. His concern with literary theory was part of a larger set of enquiries into the very nature of aesthetics, experience and their ethical dimensions.

Bakhtin held academic positions in relatively unknown provincial towns throughout his life. In the 1930s, he was in political exile in Kazakhstan. Mordovia, where he took up a post teaching literature at the State Pedagogical Institute from 1936 to 1937, was another remote place. During the Second World War, he was forced to live in anonymity, fearing the Stalinist repression. Bakhtin taught at local schools for a living, visiting Moscow occasionally, for his research. He returned to his teaching post in Mordovia after the war, and retired from there in 1961. Though he continued to write all through these years, he hardly published anything worthwhile. He completed work on 'Discourse in the Novel' during 1930–36. He worked on the bildungsroman project, 'Forms of Time and of the Chronotope in the Novel' and the dissertation on Rabelais during 1937–39. The dissertation was ready by 1940. Bakhtin defended his dissertation at the Gorky Institute on 15 November 1946 but was denied the degree of Doctor of Philological Sciences. In June 1952, he was awarded a lower degree, the degree of Candidate of Philological Sciences, which ended his hopes of securing a career at a reputed university.

Considering the fact that Bakhtin worked at obscure places, in complete anonymity, it is nothing short of a miracle that he was discovered by a new generation of readers in the 1960s and brought back into the limelight. Sergei Georgievich Bocharov, Vadim Kozhinov and Georgii Gachev, the young scholars who saved him from oblivion, visited him in February 1961. By September 1963, a revised edition of *Problems of Dostoevsky's Poetics* appeared. Bakhtin's book on Rabelais, which was published in 1965, was hailed as a classic. A collection of his essays on the novel, *The Dialogic Imagination*, appeared in 1975, the year he died.

Any study of Mikhail Bakhtin is bound to run into a series of problems related to his enormous corpus spread across diverse areas ranging from linguistics to philosophy. Bakhtin was not consistent in his thought and writing as his interests were varied. There is also confusion about the authorship of some of the texts that have been published under the names of scholars who were part of the Bakhtin Circle. Bakhtin lived during unsettled times, frequently shifting base, and was forced to live in exile for long periods, away from Moscow. All this has given rise to a complex publication history, with Bakhtin's early books appearing in English much later, and his later books making their way to Europe and America only in the 1970s.

DISPUTED AUTHORSHIP

The disputed authorship of some of the works of members of the Bakhtin Circle has been a matter of great controversy ever since it came to light in the 1970s. For instance, Bakhtin's friend, Ivan Kanaev, had introduced him to developments in biology. Following this, Bakhtin wrote a long review-article titled 'Contemporary Vitalism', which was published in 1926 under the name of Ivan Kanaev. The review has since been correctly attributed to Bakhtin, after Kanaev acknowledged that it was authored by Bakhtin. However, the publications under the names of Medvedev and Voloshinov which have been attributed to Bakhtin were not similarly authenticated. Hence, it is only speculation that the books published under the names of these two authors were really written by Bakhtin. Both Medvedev and Voloshinov died in the 1930s, and thus we have no means of establishing the truth of the matter. The authorship of *The Formal Method in Literary Scholarship: A Critical Introduction to Sociological Poetics* (1928) by Medvedev and that of the two books by Voloshinov, *Freudianism: A Marxist Critique* (1976) and *Marxism and the Philosophy of Language* (1973), will forever remain in the shadow of doubt.

However, not all scholars are convinced that Bakhtin is the sole author of the books in question. What is under scrutiny is Bakhtin's relation to Marxism. Gary Morson and Caryl Emerson have argued in *Mikhail Bakhtin: Creation of a Prosaics* (1990) that the claim about Bakhtin's sole authorship is not sustainable. Both Voloshinov and Medvedev were scholars in their own right and had an impact on Bakhtin's thinking. Medvedev had a successful career as a public intellectual until he was arrested and shot in 1938 during the Stalinist purge. Voloshinov was a senior research worker at a state institute, when he died of tuberculosis in 1936. It is argued that these authors articulated a Marxian point of view in their books, which Bakhtin would not have openly identified with. Bakhtin's ambivalence towards Marxist thought was well known, and it is possible that these books were products of collaborative scholarship at a time when Bakhtin's own ideas were at a formative stage. As his early philosophical tracts demonstrate, Bakhtin's ideas were in the process of being formulated during the 1920s, and he must have shared some of the sociological views of his collaborators at this stage.

Voloshinov/Bakhtin's *Marxism and the Philosophy of Language* attracted the attention of Russian formalists like Roman Jakobson, which was the reason it was translated into French and English. The critiques of Freudianism and structuralism offered by these authors have been influential in shaping Russian thought in the 1930s. As we shall explore later, there is an underlying line of thought concerning the very nature of language that links these authors. Throughout his life, Bakhtin was concerned with the nature of language use and its inherent creative potential to question received notions of reality. He engaged with several philosophical systems of thought, including Marxism, and to classify him as anti-Marxist would be as much a distortion of facts as to describe him as committed to religion. His concerns were ethical and moral and his engagement with literary texts deepened these concerns to the point where they became primary themes in his pre-eminent books.

Bakhtin's years in exile in Kazakhstan were productive to a great extent. He completed the essay 'Discourse in the Novel', though there was not much scope of publication. It was finally published in 1975. After his exile, he was able to get an academic position in the Mordovian Pedagogical Institute in the provincial town of Saransk. He could not last long there, however, due to political interference that resulted in the termination of the Head of the institution. Bakhtin kept moving between Moscow, Leningrad and Kazakhstan, hoping to find secure employment. Ultimately, he had to survive on teaching jobs in secondary schools outside Moscow.

Many of the essays Bakhtin wrote during the 1930s and 40s, such as 'Forms of Time and the Chronotope of the Novel' and 'Epic and the Novel', were published much later or after his death in 1975. Bakhtin lived in the margins of the academy, known only to a close circle of friends and well-wishers. The only reason he survived was that he did not occupy any prominent position and did not publish much, though he continued to think and write all through the period of Stalinist purges. When speaking of Bakhtin's life, one must remember that many perished in the concentration camps or simply vanished, whereas Bakhtin managed to survive in the trying circumstances and continued to live a life of the mind despite adversities of the worst kind.

By the late 1950s, the worst of the Stalinist repression was a thing of the past. As the repressive apparatus was dismantled, those who had suffered in isolation and anonymity began to be recognised. A revised version of Bakhtin's book on Dostoevsky, *Problems of Dostoevsky's Poetics*, appeared in 1963. His unpublished dissertation on Rabelais was published in 1965, and by 1967 it was accepted that there was no underground organisation called 'Resurrection', as alleged by the Stalinist regime back in 1929. As his books began to be translated into English and French, Bakhtin came to be recognised as an important literary theorist. He was claimed by many schools such as semiotics, structuralism and Marxism, as his early works continued to appear in Russia. When he passed away in 1975, at the age of seventy-nine, Bakhtin had begun acquiring the proportions of a legend. In the subsequent decades, as some of his early works such as *The Aesthetics of Verbal Art* (1979) and *Toward a Philosophy of the Act* (1993) were published, his oeuvre became progressively complex, necessitating new assessment and evaluation.

After the collapse of the Soviet Union, more archival information on Bakhtin and his circle has become available. The Russian Academy of Sciences published the *Collected Works* of Bakhtin in six volumes between 1996 and 2012, after meticulous scrutiny of Bakhtin's original manuscripts carefully gathered from several sources. The *Collected Works* excluded the disputed works attributed to the joint authorship of Bakhtin and his friends. The editors comment, 'The authorial participation of M.M.B. in these works is beyond doubt and was affirmed by the author in conversations with different interlocutors, but it remains an open question what form the authorship and co-working with the signed authors took' (Hirschkop 20). Bakhtin's own admission in 1960 that 'in the period when these books were written we worked in very close creative contact' (qtd. in Hirschkop 19) does not resolve the issue. The period between 1924 and 1929 was politically turbulent and volatile, and Bakhtin was at a formative stage at this time, moving between philosophy, linguistics and literary criticism, involving himself in all the debates that were reshaping the directions of knowledge in humanities.

BAKHTIN'S RECEPTION IN THE WEST AND IN RUSSIA

Before providing a brief outline of the contents of this volume, a note on the reception of Bakhtin's books in Russia and the West may be in order. Many of the complications related to Bakhtin's ideas can be traced to the haphazard way in which his books appeared in the West. Bakhtin published his first book, *Problems of Dostoevsky's Art,* in 1929. His arrest in December 1929 prevented the book being discussed publicly. Between 1929 and 1963, Bakhtin could not publish any books and his ideas were known only to a small circle of friends. *Problems of Dostoevsky's Poetics* was published in 1963, followed by his work on Rabelais in 1965. He was formally rehabilitated on 30 May 1967.

Tzvetan Todorov published his study of Bakhtin in French, in 1981, and the same appeared in English translation, under the title *Mikhail Bakhtin: The Dialogical Principle* from the Minnesota University Press in the US and the Manchester University Press in London, in 1984. Julia Kristeva's essays on Bakhtin, 'The Ruin of Poetics' and 'Word, Dialogue and Novel', appeared in *Desire in Language: A Semiotic Approach to Literature and Art* published by Basil Blackwell, in 1981. Both these books made Bakhtin a familiar figure among the French critics. Strangely, he was being seen as part of the school of Russian formalism by Slavist critics during this time. Kristeva found him making a break with Russian formalism while Todorov placed him in the tradition of German Romanticism. The book on Rabelais appeared in English in 1968, from Massachusetts Institute of Technology. While some of the reviews were hostile, social historians found the book relevant to their project of 'history from below'. Two books that appeared in quick succession in English translation, *Questions of Literature and Aesthetic* (1975) and *The Aesthetics of Verbal Art* (1979), enhanced Bakhtin's reputation as a theorist in the English-speaking world. Later, it was discovered that these collections were selected and put together by the editors without much regard for continuity or comprehensiveness.

By the 1980s, the widespread interest in Deconstruction and poststructuralism had altered the field of critical approaches. With the appearance of *The Dialogic Imagination* in English in 1981, Bakhtin was added to the list of new theorists, breaking new ground in the study of narrative, linguistics and semiotics. There were 'many Bakhtins' now, depending on the school of criticism one followed. Ken Hirschkop comments, 'In the 1980s and 1990s, a hundred flowers of Bakhtin interpretation bloomed, and they were wildly different in colour and shape' (151). The Russian religious thinkers found his idea of 'Super-addressee' to be a validation of his religious beliefs; the liberal critics found 'dialogue' to be a reiteration of an underlying moral sense of human relations; and for the Leftists, Bakhtin's interest in popular culture, coupled with his emphasis on parody, irony and stylisation, enriched the discipline of cultural studies. Bakhtin's study of the novel had created a 'prosaics' of the genre, with a well-defined methodology. His accent on the non-official and the oppositional served the advocates of counter-culture across a spectrum of critical schools. The early Bakhtin of the 1920s appealed to the religious group of critics while the Bakhtin of the 1930s found favour with leftist critics.

From time to time, critics raised dissenting voices regarding the ambiguities and ambivalences in Bakhtin's positions on seminal matters. Edward Said, Paul de Man and Robert Young have noticed how 'dialogism' fits contradictory ideologies. As pointed out later in this book, Bakhtin's complex style of writing, his habit of leaving manuscripts unfinished and his unsettled life also complicated his reception.

Both feminist and postcolonial criticism found Bakhtinian concepts productive and appropriated their possibilities in multiple ways. The idea that one could subvert the ideological orientation of a discourse to embody it with voices from the margins, enabled critics to examine masculinist or colonial discourses from positions of resistance. The conflict between centrifugal and centripetal forces in the field of culture played out in several contexts in postcolonial analyses. The 'double-voiced discourse', of which Bakhtin had much to say, was particularly relevant to the manner in which novelistic narratives staged dissent in societies where the dominant power structure had assumed hegemonic status. The monologic discourse of the colonial authority reveals the presence of the other, which it tries to repress through its implicit double-voicedness. In the African-American context, the asymmetrical racial relations burdened with 'double consciousness', as W. E. B. Du Bois puts it, had given rise to a Black vernacular rich in parody, irony and carnivalised spectacles. Bakhtin's concepts had their applications in the study of the spectacular and the grotesque, particularly in performance studies and film studies.

After the previously inaccessible Bakhtin manuscripts became available, and the Russian Academy of Sciences produced Bakhtin's *Collected Works* in six volumes, there is greater clarity regarding his views and approaches. There is a gulf between the Russian Bakhtin and the English Bakhtin which will be bridged only when his *Complete Works* will become available in English. This does not invalidate the Bakhtinian interpretations that have come into circulation worldwide since the 1980s. His reception during the 1980s and 90s set the tone of the dialogic mode of criticism which has since stayed. This is unlikely to change in any substantial manner.

AN OUTLINE OF THE BOOK

A brief outline of the book is provided below, to help the reader grasp the structure and organisation of ideas and arguments presented in this volume.

Chapter two presents the basic concepts and contexts of Bakhtin, and elaborates on his approach to language. As opposed to the theoretical approach propagated by structuralist linguistics, Bakhtin views language as something fluid and unfinished, perennially in circulation in everyday use. The distinction between 'utterance' and 'sentence' is of paramount importance for Bakhtin. The dialogic orientation of the word, its contextual specificity and historical concreteness are traits that lead us to questions of interrelations between words and discourses. The centrifugal and centripetal forces that shape the field of culture show languages are pulled between stability and flux. The concepts of 'heteroglossia' and 'polyphony' are discussed in detail to bring out their nature and function in society. The novel as a genre has demonstrated its ability to embody heteroglossia and polyphony to the fullest extent, in modern times. Bakhtin collaborated closely with Voloshinov to write *Marxism and the Philosophy of Language.* The main arguments of the book are presented in this chapter. The constraints of individualistic subjectivism and abstract objectivism have crippled our ability to understand the true nature of language. These discussions take us to the very core of Bakhtin's idea of dialogism contained in the dictum, 'any true understanding is dialogic in nature' (Morris 35). Freud's theories are subjected to close analysis by Voloshinov/Bakhtin to demonstrate how their essentialist approach to concepts like sexuality, limits their ability to move beyond the theoretical. Medvedev/Bakhtin's critique of Russian formalism shows how Bakhtin's thought evolved in the 1920s.

The third chapter discusses some of the important concepts and topics Bakhtin outlined in two of his philosophical treatises, *Art and Answerability* and *Toward a Philosophy of the Act,* which belong to his early period. These books appeared in English in 1990 and 1993, respectively, though they were published in Russian between 1919 and 1924. His early works mentioned above dealt with abstract ideas of philosophy in densely written prose. The impact of neo-Kantianism in Bakhtin, outlined initially, marks an entry point into his world of philosophical ideas. This chapter delves deep into the relation between language and experience, illustrating the finer points of Bakhtin's argument with reference to the poem 'Skunk Hour' by Robert Lowell. Concepts such as 'outsideness' and 'unfinalisability' which are elaborated here, have their echoes in the later works of Bakhtin.

The fourth chapter is concerned with *Problems of Dostoevsky's Poetics,* which is considered Bakhtin's major contribution to literary criticism and the study of the novelistic genre. This book has brought into being a new critical vocabulary to analyse novelistic genres. It shows how Dostoevsky's novels realised the novel's potential to embody polyphony to the greatest extent. Students of literature will find useful Bakhtin's discussion of the double-voiced discourse and the classification of discourses of various types. To better understand

Bakhtin, it is important to follow the critical breakthrough he made in the study of Dostoevsky's novels. Since Bakhtin's reputation as a literary theorist is largely built on his study of Dostoevsky's novels, this chapter examines dialogism as a process in relation to novels like *Crime and Punishment* by Dostoevsky. Though Bakhtin's theory of chronotope is discussed separately in the sixth chapter, here the concept is illustrated with reference to Dostoevsky's novel.

Bakhtin's *Rabelais and his World*, the subject of the fifth chapter, has altered the way we look at folk and popular cultures. In this book, Bakhtin rewrote the cultural history of Europe from the perspective of popular literature. Some of his favourite ideas such as heteroglossia, unfinalisability and dissent are echoed here. His treatment of grotesque realism provides a methodology for culture studies. The language and spectacles of the market place have been transformed into new narrative modes in novelistic genres. Bakhtin also traces the history of laughter to a millennium before the Renaissance. His elaboration of grotesque realism and its many forms provided an implicit critique of the dominant mode of social realism in Soviet Russia. Bakhtin's valorisation of the carnival culture has been read as a critique of Stalinist repression in its darkest phase.

The sixth chapter is devoted to the study of Bakhtin's theories on the novel, as they evolved in his later phase. After his book on Dostoevsky, he continued to revise and refine his views on the novel and this resulted in the essays contained in *The Dialogic Imagination*, which appeared in English in 1981. By examining the development of the modern novel from the prehistory of novelistic discourses, he shows how this genre is fundamentally different from other literary genres. The novel as a genre was not theorised seriously, as it was seen as part of non-canonised literature. Bakhtin's exploration of the novel fundamentally differs from that of critics such as Georg Lukacs, Lucien Goldmann and Friedrich Engels. This becomes clear in the discussion of chronotope and its implications for the study of the novel. The chapter concludes with a note on the relation between aesthetics and ethics in relation to Bakhtin's theories of the novel.

The last chapter examines the legacy of Bakhtin for the humanities as a whole. Ideas such as intertextuality and dialogic imagination have been widely used in literary studies in various contexts. The way Bakhtin has transformed the study of popular culture is elaborated on critically. His theory of the novel enables us to see the connections between a literary genre and the power relations in society. He differs from thinkers like Foucault in the way he views the operation of power in society. This chapter illustrates the intricacies of concepts like chronotope and heteroglossia with reference to some well-known Indian novels.

Note: For the information presented in the section on 'Bakhtin's Reception in the West and in Russia', I am indebted to the book by Ken Hirschkop included in the references below.

REFERENCES

Clark, Katerina, and Michael Holquist. *Mikhail Bakhtin*. Cambridge, MA: The Belknap Press (Harvard UP), 1984. Print.

Hirschkop, Ken. *The Cambridge Introduction to Mikhail Bakhtin*. Cambridge/New York: Cambridge UP, 2021. Print.

Morris, Pam, ed. *The Bakhtin Reader: Selected Writings of Bakhtin, Medvedev, Voloshinov*. London: Arnold Publishers, 1994. Print.

Morson, Gary Saul, and Caryl Emerson. *Mikhail Bakhtin: Creation of a Prosaics*. Stanford: Stanford UP, 1990. Print.

Chapter Two

Mikhail Bakhtin: Contexts and Concepts

BASIC CONCEPTS OF BAKHTIN'S THOUGHT

The foundational elements of Bakhtin's thoughts have to be sought in his views on language as discourse and in the way the social function of language creatively informs literary genres, novelistic genres in particular. He differed from the linguist's view of language as a structured, finite entity. Language is perennially in flux, as it continually evolves as a creative medium among the common people actively engaged in communication. Attempts to regulate it, through rules regarding usage, as often laid down by academics of authority such as lexicographers and grammarians, do not impact its form or content.

Ferdinand Saussure's structuralist view of language had emphasised 'langue' as the defining feature of language in a given system, as opposed to 'parole', its everyday manifestation in actual usage. A 'langue'-centred view of language, being essentialist in nature, does not admit the orality of discourse for serious study. For Saussure, only 'langue' qualified as a legitimate area of linguistic analysis while 'parole' was too fragmentary to merit systematic study.

Saussure provided a radical insight when he said that the linguistic sign is made up of two parts: the 'signifier' that exists as the written or spoken word or a visual sign, and what it denotes, 'the signified', which exists as 'referent' or 'meaning'. Saussure further suggested that the relation between the 'signifier' and the 'signified' is arbitrary.

This opened up a whole field of study called semiology or semiotics, which entailed the detailed study of signs and their relations to their referents. A sign is ideologically loaded as its meaning is always dependent on changing contexts. Structural linguistics owes its theoretical origins to Saussure's basic insights into the structure of language. It led to the scientific study of language, its formal features and deep structures.

Bakhtin's own thinking was shaped in the context of 'the linguistic turn' that followed Saussure's path-breaking studies on the nature of language. This led to the dominance of the scientific approach in the study of literature and society. Russian formalists such as Boris Eikhenbaum, Viktor Shklovsky and Vladimir Propp are notable for applying the scientific methodology to the study of literary texts. They isolated various aspects of the form and used a taxonomic method to do so and investigate them. Bakhtin was opposed to 'scientism' since such a theoretical approach assumes that a text is a homogenous and stable object that can be subjected to analysis. In *Marxism and the Philosophy of Language* (1929), Voloshinov/Bakhtin underlines the fluidity of the medium of language. He comments: 'What is important for the speaker about a linguistic form is not that it is a stable and always self-equivalent signal, but that it is an always changeable and adaptable sign' (68).

Utterance

A linguistic sign is inherently unstable and any attempt to standardise it and finalise its semantic content is an injustice to the fundamental nature of language. This is where the distinction between 'utterance' and 'sentence' becomes crucial in Bakhtin's theory of language. For Bakhtin, 'language in use' as discourse is the more fundamental aspect of language, as it gives rise to 'living language'. He makes a fundamental distinction between 'utterance' and 'sentence'. An utterance is a unit of speech or written communication, and demands a response. An utterance could consist of a single word or a sound like 'Oh!' or it could be as long as an entire epic. It is distinguished from a 'sentence', which is a grammatical unit of language that exists without a social context. Utterances are not repeatable as they are context-bound. Words do not obey the directives of the dictionary as far as meanings are concerned, since, in actual practice, meanings are produced by the context of their use. The intonation or accent of a word or phrase determines what it means. Meanings carry with them evaluations of their content, and this further renders context paramount in the construction of meaning. Bakhtin holds that meaning is a becoming, a future possibility. Meanings cannot be fixed in time or space. In all his major works, Bakhtin's focus is on discourse, language in use, rather than on language as an abstract system of rules.

An utterance anticipates a response, and to that extent it is an event in a communicative process. A speaker in the communicative process is socially constituted and historically situated, hence, the utterance cannot be understood or explained without reference to their concrete situations. The situation enters into utterance as a necessary constitutive element. The spatio-temporal horizon of an utterance frames its meaning. Its orientation towards the listener—the other—is present even when the other is absent. It is in this sense that all utterances become dialogic.

For Bakhtin, we are always in *medias res,* in the process of a dialogue, with no possibility of a last word. Culture is nothing but a collective memory of discourses where the voices of others, including those who lived in the past, are always present. When meanings are considered final, it leads to semantic closure, rendering discourses monologic. The dialogism of the word renders it profoundly intertextual. As the word is oriented towards its answer, it fulfils itself only in the context of another word, making each word bond with its other into an intertextual relation. When this happens in a literary text, the voice of the other penetrates a given text, rendering it open and polysemic.

Centrifugal and Centripetal Forces in Culture

Bakhtin recognises that all cultures tend towards stability and order. Centripetal forces (those moving towards the centre) work in favour of stasis, sameness and unity. As opposed to this, centrifugal forces (those moving away from the centre) work towards diversity, flux and constant changes. The conflict between centripetal and centrifugal forces is visible everywhere in the cosmos, from the human body to entire civilisations. In Western tradition, philosophers such as Aristotle, Descartes and Hegel have advocated orderly systems, moving away from the flux of life and the world. On the other hand, there are thinkers such as Heraclitus and Levinas, who considered historical flux the necessary condition of human life. Bakhtin finds that language is also pulled in opposite directions by centrifugal and centripetal forces. Institutions like the Academy and their efforts to standardise languages result in the imposition of normative regimes. This is, however, resisted by the inherent creativity of languages. As we shall see later in his theory of carnivalesque forms, Bakhtin shows how the market place is a theatre for languages to flourish in all their diversity. Creative literature breaks the linguistic order imposed by regimes of centralised authority.

Heteroglossia

Language is both a cognitive system and a social practice, but it is the role of language as social practice that Bakhtin focuses on. A stable, unified language is often a requirement in a nation state which regulates culture. The conflict between official and unofficial discourses makes all national cultures a theatre of opposing tendencies. Bakhtin uses the term 'heteroglossia' to denote the inherent plurality of a language in its social form. Language exists in diverse forms since authoritarian rule cannot achieve linguistic homogeneity in a society. Apart from various dialects, language also exists in numerous registers, from its high-flown, elitist format to the common varieties spoken in the streets. At the level of utterance, it is to be recognised that traces of past and future utterances are contained in the present utterance.

While literary genres use the potential of linguistic plurality to varying extents, it is the novelistic form which has been able to represent 'heteroglossia' in its most complex form. Heteroglossia is a reflection of the internal differentiation of a society. Differences in class, gender, race, caste and region—not to mention religion and political beliefs—give rise to various modes of discourses and this is the stuff of which 'heteroglossia' is made. The novel as a literary form has been particularly successful in realising the condition of heteroglossia in its very formalistic structure.

Heteroglossia refers to the internal stratification of a country's language into several 'dialects'. Apart from dialects, there are linguistic differences across castes, classes, generations, social groups and also across professions. Dialects are filled with the worldviews of their speakers. As we shall see later, heteroglossia is a social phenomenon which is central to the genre of the novel. Polyglossia refers to the plurality of national languages which impact each other across their boundaries to produce a state of 'multi-languagedness'. If languages remain in isolation, they will never be influenced by each other. Bakhtin believes that no language has ever flourished in total isolation. It is in the nature of languages to borrow from each other and learn from each other. Heteroglossia is the underlying condition of every language. R. B. Kershner explains this condition as follows:

> For Bakhtin, both written and spoken languages and inner monologue are made up of a great variety of conflicting variants—languages of officialdom, vernaculars, occupational jargons, technical, literary, and sub-literary languages, all polyphonically resounding. . . . The condition of our existence is thus heteroglossia, a conflicting multiplicity of languages; dialogism is the necessary mode of knowledge in such a world, a form of relationship between or among different languages that, like dialectics, defines a sort of language. (15–16)

As the language is caught between the centripetal and centrifugal forces of culture, it is always in a state of becoming. Literary language is one of the many languages that exists in a language. The condition of heteroglossia is dynamic as it is constantly being shaped by social forces outside. To study a language, it is not enough to examine its grammatical system, one needs to study its internal social stratifications. Bakhtin was aware that heteroglossia reflects the power structures in society which are in a state of struggle. In this respect, Bakhtin anticipates some of the concepts put forward by Foucault many decades later.

Polyphony

It is important to distinguish heteroglossia from the concept of 'polyphony'. In his study of Dostoevsky's novels, Bakhtin showed how they are multi-voiced. This means that the author's point of view does not dominate the narrative, suppressing and sidelining the voices of the characters. The protagonist is subjected to the same treatment as the minor characters, his/her consciousness is subjected to alterations in relation to the characters he/she interacts with. In such a narrative, the multiple voices of the community or society become manifest in the very structure of the novel. The novel makes it possible for readers to listen to the voice of the minor characters, as they are not controlled and silenced by the author or the main characters. The consciousnesses of characters constantly interpenetrate in the narrative, making it possible for the multiple voices to be heard. It was in Dostoevsky's novels that the condition of heteroglossia found its full expression. Polyphony results from the clash between multiple ideological worlds represented through the discourses in a novel.

The unitary language of official authority loses its centrality and sanctity in the novelistic form as official discourses are subjected to critical examination from the margins. A narrative where only the protagonist's voice is heard will be monologic, creating a privileged domain of meanings. This is where the Dostoevskian novel stands apart. In creating the polyphonic novel, Dostoevsky created an ideological form that answers to the inherent dialogic potential of language and society. We will examine Bakhtin's analysis of Dostoevsky's novels in detail in a subsequent chapter.

Intertextuality is another feature of the polyphonic narrative. When words are inhabited by others' voices, they become oriented towards the other, establishing a relation of reciprocities. This will be a recurring subject in our discussion.

A Marxist Theory of Language

The question of language remained a central concern for Bakhtin throughout his career as a literary theorist and thinker. Hence, it is necessary to elaborate on the foundational ideas that animate his system of thought. Voloshinov's essay 'Discourse in Life and Discourse in Poetry' (1926) and his book *Marxism and the Philosophy of Language* will figure in this discussion prominently as we view them as collaborative works where Bakhtin's ideas were incorporated into the main arguments. During the 1920s, linguistics was a highly influential discipline in Russia. Ferdinand Saussure's *A Course in General Linguistics* (1916) ushered in a linguistic turn in the disciplines of literary criticism and philosophy. Saussure's meticulous delineation of language as a system made it possible to study language scientifically. The work of Russian formalists demonstrated how literature came to be studied from a linguistic point of view. Literature was no longer viewed simply in relation to the psychological features of the author. In the 1920s, the Marxist approach which emphasised the social function of literature was gaining ground, but it was yet to assume the hegemonic status it attained in the Stalinist era.

Voloshinov/Bakhtin identifies two trends that obstruct the proper understanding of language as an object of study, namely, individualistic subjectivism and abstract objectivism. When we consider 'the individual creative act of speech' as the basis of language, we trace everything to the individual psyche (Morris 26). The other trend consists of reducing language to 'a system of the phonetic, grammatical and lexical forms of language' (26). In this view, language becomes a closed system which does not enable us to comprehend its nature as a living, historical phenomenon. Voloshinov/Bakhtin writes: 'Abstract objectivism finds its most striking expression at the present time in the so-called Geneva School of Ferdinand de Saussure' (29). They further note that the majority of Russian thinkers in linguistics are influenced by Saussure and his disciples in a determinative way. While distinguishing 'langue' from 'parole', Saussure finds the former to be central while the latter is seen as peripheral, or more or less random.

For Saussure, 'utterance' is an 'individual act of will and intelligence' where the codified system of language is utilised by the individual for 'expressing his own personal thoughts' (31). Saussure's main thesis, according to Voloshinov, is: 'Language stands in opposition to utterance in the same way as does that which is social to that which is individual' (31). This also means that utterance cannot be a proper subject of study. This is where Voloshinov/Bakhtin finds it necessary to offer a critique of Saussurean linguistics, arguing that language as an abstract system does not, in any way, determine the nature of utterance:

'The speaker's subjective consciousness does not in the least operate with language as a system of normatively identical forms' (32).

Language in use is always the product of a concrete context. What is valuable in the use of language is its ability to express the intention of the speaker, his/her point of view. Understanding an utterance does not imply following its linguistic structure but capturing what is new and changeable in the given set of words. Here, Voloshinov makes a distinction between a sign and a signal; a sign can be understood only through interpretation, whereas a signal is always recognised as something having a fixed and finite meaning, as in the red light at a traffic signal. A sign, on the other hand, relates to the domain of the ideological. The speaker is not concerned with the language as an abstract system. Voloshinov/Bakhtin comments: 'In actuality, we never say or hear *words,* we say and hear what is true or false, good or bad, important or unimportant, pleasant or unpleasant, and so on' (33). In ordinary situations we are not even conscious of the grammatical correctness of an utterance as long as it communicates to us.

When we dislodge language from its ideological domain, we reduce it to a lifeless entity with no relation to any living community. Extreme forms of 'theoreticism' result in a reductive view of language as inert, passive and closed, and not as dynamic, creative and active, and this denies it the power to intervene in the shaping of human worlds. Voloshinov/Bakhtin shifts the emphasis of linguistic study from 'langue' to 'parole', from a codified system of rules to utterance and discourse. It is in the nature of utterance to anticipate a response. An utterance is related to all utterances, and in this sense, it is part of an unbroken chain of speech performances. Voloshinov/Bakhtin believes that the question of meaning is one of the most difficult problems in linguistics. We can understand another's utterance only if we are oriented towards it. We should be able to situate ourselves in the context of the other's utterance. Social situations and evaluative judgements are intrinsic to exchanges between individuals.

One of the defining principles of Bakhtin's idea of language is postulated here when he says 'Any true understanding is dialogic in nature' (35). Meaning does not belong to a single word, but to a 'word in its position between speakers' (35). In the process of active, responsive understanding, meaning is realised as part of the performance of speech as an interpersonal event.

Voloshinov/Bakhtin also argues that a word conveys its meaning through its evaluative accent. This means that a word incorporates within it a value judgement. This is communicated through the 'expressive intonation' of the word. Here, it must be remembered that utterance implies a wide range of discourses, from everyday speech to a complex literary text, such as a lyric, an epic or a novel. The 'reader' of the literary text is like the 'listener' in a real-life communication scenario. A literary work comes into being as an intertextual dialogue with another literary work. Similarly, non-literary speech varieties of a society are also part of the context of a literary work. In a literary work, the social worlds of the characters, the author and the reader enter into a dialogue, their consciousnesses fuse into a single horizon, making it possible for them to participate in a communicative event.

By focusing on the abstract system of language, we cannot infer the meaning of an utterance. This is because the process of understanding involves evaluation. A speaker or a listener chooses a particular meaning from the available range of meanings, based on his/her perception of context and intonation of the utterance. A change in meaning is the result of a re-evaluation. A word moves from a particular evaluative context to another, demanding a change in perception of meaning. A particular social group will have an evaluative view that determines the generation of meaning within the group. Voloshinov/Bakhtin observes: 'Society in the process of generation expands its perception of the generative process of existence. There is nothing in this that could be said to be absolutely fixed' (37). Meanings are caught in the contradictions of a living society, where new conditions of existence demand constant changes and re-evaluations.

The term 'translinguistics' or 'metalinguistics' has been used to describe Bakhtin's conceptual approach to language. Elements of language such as phonetics, syntax and grammar shape the communication process. Bakhtin's 'Discourse in Life and Discourse in Art' (1926) articulates the approach which he refined in his later works in different forms. The fundamental difference between the study of scientific subjects and the study of language is sociological in nature. Voloshinov/Bakhtin explains it in lucid terms:

> Social definitions are not applicable from outside, as is the case with bodies and substances in nature—*ideological formations are intrinsically, immanently sociological*. . . . The most subtle formal nuances of a law or of a political system are all equally amenable to the sociological method and only to it. But exactly the same thing is true for other ideological forms. They are all *sociological through and through,* even though their structure, mutable and complex as it is, lends itself to exact analysis only with enormous difficulty. (*Freudianism* 95)

What is of consequence here is the basic assumption that art, aesthetic and philosophy cannot be understood outside the sociological matrix of their formations. To interpret art and aesthetic one has to enter the world of the social. Earlier, it was believed that meaning emanates from the content of verbal communication alone and its context is not of great significance. Bakhtin insists that details like the social location of the speaker, the tone of communication, the ideological content of the message, the accompanying gestures help shape the meaning of what is communicated.

In a famous example, Voloshinov mentions two people facing each other in a room. One man says, 'Well.' It is impossible to deduce the meaning of this utterance, as it has no semantic content. However, if you are told that the two were looking out of the window and were reacting to the snowy weather outside, the statement becomes immediately intelligible. The meaning is provided by the context of the speakers. Since the context decides the meaning in every utterance, for Bakhtin, no utterance can be repeated. The meaning will change with changing contexts. The intonation and the gesture accompanying an utterance decides its orientation, and conveys whether it was spoken in jest, or in exclamation or anger, and so on. And this will further alter the meaning.

In *Marxism and the Philosophy of Language,* Voloshinov/Bakhtin outlines the dialogic nature of understanding. A word points in two directions, in the direction of the speaker and that of the listener. The meaning is not inherent in the word, but it unfolds in the act of communication when it is accompanied by a series of extra-linguistic features. Understanding is a dialogic process as the meaning is realised only as part of a process of communication. As mentioned above, the evaluative function of extra-linguistic elements such as intonation, gestures and situation need to be taken into account in interpreting a word.

The Problem of Reported Speech

The relation between the speaker and the listener becomes important when the speech is received and further transmitted. Reported speech is a document of reception, indicating the social tendencies that operate in language forms. It is not a matter of individual preference but a social tendency. Reported speech affirms the dialogic nature of language. It shows that dialogue as an organising principle of meaning can be studied with reference to syntax. The difference between direct and indirect speech lies in its active reception by a third person, for whom it is intended. Further, the context of this transmission also impacts the reported speech. Voloshinov/Bakhtin observes: 'Between the reported speech and reporting context, dynamic relations of high complexity and tension are in force' (119). Analysing the tendencies in the relationships between reporting and reported speech, a certain evolution in their nature and function has been noted by Voloshinov/Bakhtin, and is represented as follows:

1. *Authoritarian dogmatism*, characterized by the linear, impersonal, monumental style of reported speech transmission in the Middle Ages;
2. *Rationalistic dogmatism,* with its even more precise linear style in the 17th and 18th centuries;
3. *Realistic and critical individualism*, with its pictorial style and its tendency to permeate reported speech with authorial report and commentary (end of the 18th century and early 19th century); and finally,
4. *Relativistic individualism*, with its decomposition of the authorial context (the present period). (123)

The changing social conditions of the past centuries seem to have influenced the nature of relationships between direct speech and its reception. The shifting paradigms in the nature of reported speech point to the changing equations of power within the social domain. As we shall see later, the emergence of the novel cannot be understood without reference to the secular–modern social order that came into being in the wake of the Enlightenment.

Free Indirect Discourse

There are many ways in which one can receive another's speech. One can directly speak about someone or quote another's speech (quoted speech), or one can indirectly quote another's speech (indirect discourse). We can also have a discourse where one's speech merges and fuses with the other's. Bakhtin/Voloshinov describes this as 'quasi-direct speech'. It is also known as 'free indirect discourse'. In this form, two utterances are brought into a dialogic relationship: 'The dyke ruptures, as it were, and authorial intonations freely stream into the reported speech' (146). Only in the absolutely objective kind of scientific writing does the declaratory word remain predominant. Bakhtin/Voloshinov strongly argues that in all other writings it is free indirect discourse that predominates: 'All verbal activity in these cases amounts to piecing together "other persons' words" and "words seemingly from other persons"' (159).

Citing the example of Middle French, Bakhtin/Voloshinov points out that seldom does the narrator immerse himself/herself in another's speech. The two discourses remain distinctly apart: 'Reported speech becomes impersonal, and colorless, and the narrator's voice is now heard more distinctly in it than the voice of the reported speaker' (151). During the Renaissance period, we find that the narrator tries to 'align himself with his character' as greater intimacy develops between the two. A harmonious balance between the subjective and the objective is finally established only in the seventeenth century.

What characterises free indirect discourse is the quality of empathy. The author makes his/her character stand out as a responsible partner in the narrative: 'The author is able to present the utterances of his characters in a way suggesting that he himself takes them seriously, and that what is at stake is not merely something that was said or thought, but actual facts' (150). In direct discourse such empathy is missing. Indirect discourse tended to be 'too analytical and inert' (151). But free indirect discourse 'neatly surmounted the dualism of abstract analysis and unmediated impression'. In the work of an author like Jean de La Fontaine (1621–95), one can discern this balance and empathy in his retelling of fables.

The use of free indirect discourse defines a position where the author is both inside and outside his characters. Bakhtin/Voloshinov, quoting Gertraud Lerch, illustrates this with reference to the narrative perspective found in Flaubert's work. Flaubert focuses on those experiences which are repulsive and revolting. But there is a degree of empathy in his approach to these experiences. Bakhtin/Voloshinov comments: 'Quasi-direct discourse, with its capacity for conveying simultaneously identification with and independence, distance from one's creations, was an extremely suitable means for embodying this love-hate relation Flaubert maintained toward his characters' (152).

The triumph of scientific thought in all fields of life led to the gradual ascent of the declarative word in the early twentieth century. Bakhtin/Voloshinov's critique is directed against this epistemological crisis. He believes that the current stage can be characterised as 'the stage of transformation of the word into a thing, the stage of depression in the thematic value of the word' (159). Formalistic movements in poetics, linguistics and the philosophy of language are responsible for this state of things. The ideological word which is permeated with the voice of the other needs to be revived to counter this inert, scientific approach. 'The word permeated with confident and categorical social value judgement, the word that really means and takes responsibility for what it says' alone can articulate the human predicament of a living society (159).

CRITIQUE OF FREUDIANISM

If we go through the critique of Freudianism offered by Voloshinov/Bakhtin, we may find common threads from the arguments outlined above. Freud's 'biological person' is seen as an abstraction, as it is the individual as a social being who is subjected to psychological study. He/She is constituted as a social being through his/her location in a class or a place and cannot be understood in the abstract merely as an object of scientific study. Voloshinov/Bakhtin argues that Freud's psychological constructs are based on interpretation of verbal utterances. In Freud's elucidation of psychical conflict, the utterances do not directly embody the unconscious. As Voloshinov/Bakhtin observes, 'we hear only the biased voice of the subjective consciousness interpreting human behavior' (*Freudianism* 40). The social interrelationships between the patient and the doctor are never taken into account in Freud's study. These interrelationships shape the utterances of the patient. Freud bases all his observations on these utterances without taking into account how these utterances are mediated by the social. The 'psychical experiences of the speaker' are in reality 'projections' of social interrelationships into the individual's psyche. There is a wider social field of communication that decides the orientation of an individual speaker, as the language exists as a preordained social reality into which an individual is assimilated as he/she becomes a social being. In studying the patient's unconscious, Freud relies on their childhood memories. The construct of the complexes is derived from the interpretation of the remembrances of the adults. But these remembrances are nothing but 'the interpretation of the past from the point of view of the present' (42). Voloshinov/Bakhtin observes: 'We see in the past only what is important for the present, important for the instant in which we remember our past' (42). Over a period of our socialisation, we internalise ideological–evaluative interpretations of concepts such as 'love', 'sexual attraction', 'motherhood', 'father-figure', and so on. They belong to our conscious adult present, not our childhood or our unconscious. Bakhtin observes: 'Thus, *the whole of Freud's psychical dynamics is given in the ideological illumination of consciousness. Consequently, it is not a dynamics of psychical forces, but only a dynamics of various motives of consciousness*' (Morris 40).

All this leads us to conclude that concepts like the 'Oedipus Complex' are a 'purely ideological formulation' that are 'projected into the psyche of a child' (*Freudianism* 43). If we take away from Freud's formulations the evaluative tone and the ideological weight they gain in the context of adult consciousness, all that is left will be a series of disjointed observations regarding infantile sexuality and the child's attraction towards the mother. They will not constitute a coherent system of meaning. There is a chasm between what is apprehended as a series of facts and the subsequent interpretation that is built upon those facts. Freudian constructs are arbitrary and have no base in the reality of objective facts.

While we may find Voloshinov/Bakhtin's rejection of Freudian breakthrough exaggerated, we need to grant that their critique is directed against the essentialist ways in which concepts like 'sexuality' are conceived in psychoanalysis. Bakhtin's critique is directed against the discursive component of Freud's theoretical constructs. The evaluations and points of view that belong to the present are projected into the past, to project a grandiose system without taking into account the role of language in constructing reality. Voloshinov/Bakhtin underlines the need to view these as social constructs, an idea which has been further explored by critics like Michel Foucault in his studies of sexuality.

FORMAL METHOD IN LITERARY SCHOLARSHIP

The Formal Method in Literary Scholarship (1928) was jointly written by P. N. Medvedev and Bakhtin to outline the basic features of literature as a category. Medvedev/Bakhtin puts forth the complex negotiations between Marxist philosophy and literature to conclude that 'meaning' arises out of social communication. Different spheres of human activity such as art, science, ethics or religion share the same sociological laws of development. To develop a Marxian method of sociological analysis of ideological fields, the peculiarities of each ideological system should be studied. The definitions provided by Western idealistic philosophy are not adequate. Works of art, scientific works, religious symbols and rites have meanings and values embodied in material things and actions. They can be objectively grasped and described. The consciousness of a given society is shaped by the social and economic conditions of that society. The nature of upbringing and education, the cultural environment and prevailing social systems contribute towards the ideological make-up of a society.

How is literature connected to the study of ideologies? Literature refracts the determining reality of the socio-economic base, like all other ideologies. Apart from this, the content of literature also refracts the reflections and refractions of those other branches of ideology. Literary critics tend to see only one side of literature, viewing it as a reflection of the social reality outside. What they fail to see is how literature itself becomes social reality in its own right. Literature is on par with other fields of human activities such as science, ethics, epistemology, political doctrines, and religion, among others, as a phenomenon with its own ideology. When we read a play like *Antigone,* for instance, we are confronting life refracted through ideology. However, the Russian literary critics tended to reduce the complex relationship of literature and social meaning to the ideological horizon alone. They disregarded the fact that any item of social meaning, when it enters a work of art, is transformed in becoming part of an artistic whole. The contents were equated with various types of ideologies, while the artistic form was seen as a mere shell housing these ideologies. Illustrating their arguments with the novel, Medvedev/Bakhtin comments in *The Formal Method in Literary Scholarship*:

> The reality of a novel, its contact with actuality, and its role in social life cannot be reduced to the mere reflection of reality in its content. It is part of social life and active in it precisely as a novel, and, as such, sometimes has an extremely important place in social reality, a place sometimes no less important than that of the social phenomena it reflects. (Morris 132)

Only Marxism can provide us with the correct philosophical direction and methodological precision to analyse the problems raised above. A literary work is part of material reality and has its own history.

What is the relationship between the individual work and the determining ideological horizon? A work is a product of a literary environment of a particular epoch and a social group. This literary environment, in turn, is determined by the larger ideological environment of society. The ideological environment and the socio-economic environment have a dialectical relationship. Literary histories need to trace the mutual influences and interconnections between the two domains which are apparently separate, but deeply connected underneath. Medvedev/Bakhtin writes:

> The work cannot be understood outside the unity of literature. But this whole unity and the individual works which are its elements cannot be understood outside the unity of ideological life. And this last unity, whether it is taken as a whole, or separate elements, cannot be studied outside the socio-economic laws of development. (Morris 133)

There is a larger literary environment that gives rise to individual works of art. As an ideological event, a literary work is shaped by external and internal forces. The intrinsic forces are the product of larger extrinsic forces and the literary historian has to study the interrelations between these two domains, not as independent entities but mutually connected fields. What appears individual and autonomous on the surface, is, on closer examination, an ideological phenomenon with deep roots in the entire social, political and economic structures of society.

This chapter has explained the context of Bakhtin as a Russian thinker. Some of the basic ideas that form the foundational rubric of his philosophy and literary critical thinking, particularly those concerned with language and its social functions, have been discussed in detail. It is also argued that the critique of abstract objectivism of linguistics and psychoanalysis provides a ground for his future thinking on the ethical content of literary genres. In the next chapter, we will take up for detailed study, Bakhtin's philosophical ideas about the artistic process, the concept of answerability, the author–hero relations in the aesthetic activity, and some of the issues concerning language and experience. The insights he offers into the 'novelisation' of genres, or the 'novelness' of genres, follows from his perceptive analysis of the birth and development of various types of literary genres.

REFERENCES

Holquist, Michael. 'Answering as Authoring: Mikhail Bakhtin's Trans-Linguistics.' *Bakhtin: Essays and Dialogues on His Work*. Ed. Gary Saul Morson. Chicago: U of Chicago P, 1990. 59–71. Print.

Kershner, R. B. *Joyce, Bakhtin and Popular Literature: Chronicles of Disorder.* Chapel Hill: U of North Carolina P, 1989. Print.

Morris, Pam, ed. *The Bakhtin Reader: Selected Writings of Bakhtin, Medvedev, Voloshinov.* London: Arnold Publishers, 1994. Print.

Voloshinov, V. N./Bakhtin, M. M. *Marxism and the Philosophy of Language.* Trans. Ladislav Matejka and I. R. Titunik. Cambridge, MA: Harvard UP, 1986. Print.

---. Trans. I. R. Titunik. *Freudianism: A Marxist Critique*. UK: Academic Press, 1976. Print.

Chapter Three

From Answerability to Unfinalisability

BAKHTIN'S PHILOSOPHICAL IDEAS ON THE ARTISTIC PROCESS

As mentioned earlier, the English translations of Bakhtin's books did not appear in the same order in which they were written in Russian. This chapter will discuss some of the important concepts and topics outlined by Bakhtin in two of his philosophical treatises, *Art and Answerability* and *Toward a Philosophy of the Act*, both of which belong to his early period. These books appeared in English in 1990 and 1993 respectively, though they were published in Russian between 1919 and 1924. Bakhtin's later works such as *Problems of Dostoevsky's Poetics* (1984) and *Rabelais and His World* (1968, 1984) appeared in English translation first. They presented critical readings of fictional works from a radical perspective which brought out the philosophical dimensions of these fictional narratives. They set a new benchmark for textual criticism of fiction in the twentieth century and marked a major breakthrough in the field of literary criticism. However, his early works mentioned above dealt with abstract ideas of philosophy in densely written prose. They have a significant bearing on Bakhtin's later development and cannot be excluded from his framework of ideas. Chronologically, these ideas precede Bakhtin's major works which established him as a literary theorist. Since it is necessary to be familiar with his theoretical oeuvre before discussing these major works, an attempt is made here to bring out the nature of his theoretical concerns in his early works.

IMPACT OF NEO-KANTIANISM ON BAKHTIN'S THOUGHT

In these early works, Bakhtin addresses issues of self and the other as a primary distinction that informs all human relationships. Its nature can only be understood through the analysis of various binaries such as mind and reality, self and experience, time and space, and so on. His focus is on everyday experience and the manner in which we relate to the other in our daily lives. The question of ethics becomes central for Bakhtin as it underlines the world of everyday interactions. The relation between art and life was widely debated in Russia during the 1920s. Those whose allegiance lay in formalism challenged the primacy of the sociological approach in the interpretation of art. Bakhtin moves away from both the formalist and sociological approaches to develop a new vocabulary of criticism rooted in philosophical theory.

Neo-Kantian ideas played a vital role in shaping Bakhtin's new approach. In the wake of the Russian Revolution of 1919, fundamental questions concerning the nature of art and experience and their relation to knowledge had assumed greater urgency. The Marburg School of Philosophy was a major centre of learning in Europe during the early 1920s; and Russian scholars closely interacted with the academics of the Marburg School. Hermann Cohen (1842–1918), who taught at the Philosophy department at Marburg, was one of the most influential philosophers in Germany and Russia from the 1880s to the 1920s. He outlined a new set of principles to explain the relations between the human mind and the world, as well as language and reality. These ideas had an impact on the development of Bakhtin's conceptual world. His interest in art and answerability must be viewed against the larger framework of neo-Kantian ideas which were popular at Saint Petersburg University during Bakhtin's student days. His friend Matvei Kagan had studied under Hermann Cohen, who was known for his reinterpretation of Kantian ideas. Ernst Cassirer, whose well-known book *The Philosophy of Symbolic Forms* (1923–29) dwelt on issues of language and representation, was another philosopher Bakhtin followed closely.

The Marburg circle extended and refined some of the Kantian formulations regarding the relation between concepts and the empirical world. This was an attempt to challenge the positivist worldview which had gained ground by the end of the nineteenth century. Positivism upheld a scientific approach based on empirical evidence. It did not recognise the humanities or social sciences as legitimate sources of knowledge. Neo-Kantianism returned to Kant to re-emphasise a value system based on the human mind and its capacity for conceptual thinking. Do concepts exist independent of the empirical world? For Kant, 'things-in-themselves' ('*noumena*') remain beyond the reach of man's concepts and cannot be known by the human mind. Neo-Kantians found Kant's idea of 'critical or transcendental idealism' a source of several insights regarding epistemology. For Kant, knowledge is the process through which our minds give form to appearances. The human mind has certain conceptual frameworks which regulate the production of knowledge. All scientific knowledge is a combination of what is given in our first-hand experience of the empirical world and the conceptual framework that operates in the mind. For instance, our sense of space and time conditions our sensory experience. This sense of space and time that exists in us prior to our thought, contributes to the generation of knowledge. The idea that every event has a cause also seems to be central to the production of knowledge. For Kant, the mind shapes the world by combining these a priori concepts with our experiences of the world. Sensibility (the capacity for feeling) and understanding (the capacity for intellectual thought), both of which are a priori forms, become the conditions for the possibility of knowledge. Knowledge is produced when the world conforms to the requirements of human sensibility and rationality.

ART AND ANSWERABILITY

Some of the ideas discussed above will be echoed in the following discussion on Bakhtin's early conceptual world. In the brief note titled 'Art and Answerability' (1919), one of his earliest published pieces, Bakhtin affirms the need for the artist and the human being to become integrated in one person. The very first quote he uses in this essay is taken from Kant's *The Metaphysics of Morals* (1797). The three domains of human culture, namely science, art and life, need to be integrated within one person. Often their relations are mechanical. Bakhtin writes, 'But what guarantees the inner connection of the constituent elements of a person? Only the unity of answerability' (*Art and Answerability* 1). Both the artist and the individual have a common responsibility towards recognising the separate claims of art and life without reducing the other to a subsidiary role. Often, art becomes a refuge from life and life exists with no concern for art. This is where Bakhtin posits the need for answerability in life. This means that a certain balance must be struck between life and art: 'I have to answer with my own life for what I have experienced and understood in art, so that everything I have experienced and understood would not remain ineffectual in my life' (2). This mutual answerability also entails mutual liability to blame. Only by becoming completely answerable, can one integrate the different constituent elements of his life within oneself. Often 'inspiration' is invoked to suggest the aloofness of art from life. But inspiration cannot justify lack of answerability. Bakhtin observes, 'Inspiration that ignores life and is itself ignored by life is not inspiration, but a state of possession' (2). Creativity that does not recognise the claims of life as well as life that does not consider the claims of art, are both impoverished. They are ethically hollow. Art and life can become one only 'in the unity of their answerability' (2). As such, they have to be responsible for each other.

AUTHOR AND HERO IN AESTHETIC ACTIVITY

In his essay, 'Author and Hero in Aesthetic Activity' (written in the early 1920s, but published in Russian only in 1979), Bakhtin examines the relation between the self and the other, using the framework of author and hero. When we deal with the other, we do not perceive the other as a whole. We are concerned with only those actions of other people which have a bearing on us. We are also unable to perceive ourselves as a whole. However, in a work of art, an artist is able to relate to his hero as a whole, as a totality. Bakhtin writes, 'At the time an author was creating, he experienced only his hero, and he put his whole essentially necessary relationship to the hero into the image of the hero' (*Art and Answerability* 7). The relationship between the author and the hero is a dynamic, vital relationship. The author is not a person, but a capacity, an energy. The author is able to see the hero in totality because he/she is situated outside the hero. In real life, we are unable to view ourselves from the outside. The author 'intonates every trait of the hero, every event of his life, every action he performs' (4), just as in real life we react to the people around us. As an aesthetic event, the author–hero relation allows us to study the relation between two consciousnesses. Bakhtin comments, 'An aesthetic event can take place only when there are two participants present; it presupposes two non-coinciding consciousnesses' (22).

A single self cannot know itself. It is in the context of the other that the self knows itself. If we compare two individuals, each one can see certain things the other cannot see. Each one has a surplus of vision in comparison with the other. This makes each person unique: 'This ever-present *excess* of my seeing, knowing, and possessing in relation to any other human being, is founded in the uniqueness and irreplaceability of my place in the world' (23). The author comes alive only in the process of creating; it is a struggle with himself/herself. Once the author steps out of this process, he/she is not able to explain or understand it. The author is part of the text, but he/she is not present in it as he/she exists in the world outside the text. The author as an ordinary person cannot offer any insight into the creative process once the creation is over, since he/she is outside it.

Bakhtin would say that 'a unified image of myself is a gift from the other'. As mentioned earlier, the 'surplus of seeing' each one of us possesses enables us to see the other from a perspective he/she has no access to. It is only through interactions that we can form an image about ourselves. A unified sense of one's personality can be gained only through the other's consciousness. One goes out to the other to come back with a self. This is because one always remains outside any representation of oneself. The author's reaction to the hero is aesthetic since it is a 'reaction to the whole of the hero as a human being' (5). The constituents of a work attain an artistic whole through the author's capacity to objectify his/her relation with the hero, but this is done with empathy. The author remains outside the hero with reference to space and time, value and meaning. After the author projects himself/herself into the hero, he/she returns to his/her own place outside their horizon. Creation can begin only when the author enters the other and returns to himself/herself.

Authorship as metaphor and reality enables Bakhtin to examine the nature of the range of relations implied by the self and the other. Clark and Holquist comment, 'Authorship is the primary activity of all selves in a world dominated by the self/other distinction. As such, it is the ground of not only these categories but of all the other dyads around which Bakhtin's work is organized. Self and other lie behind other characteristic dichotomies such as finalized/unfinalized, official/unofficial, monologic/dialogic, epic/novel, and inner/outer' (94).

The 'excess' of seeing which privileges an author enables him/her to attain such a totality. However, Bakhtin also suggests that the self remains 'unfinalizable'. To represent the 'whole hero', the hero must be dead to the author. He writes, 'In this sense, we could say that death is the form of the aesthetic consummation of an individual' (*Art and Answerability* 131). It is important for the author to remain outside the hero, to achieve an inner understanding of the hero's life, yet not merge with him/her. This form-giving perception comes from objectivity.

Author and Hero

An author is not concerned with his/her own position in relation to the hero. He/She reflects the hero's emotional situation. His/Her own position is actualised in an object, but is not constituted as an object of enquiry. Bakhtin defines the author as 'the uniquely active, form-giving energy that is manifested . . . in a durably valid cultural product' (8). The author's presence is manifested in the art object he creates, whether it is a poem or a painting. In his discussion of 'expressive aesthetics' Bakhtin speaks of 'inner form'. Content itself creates a form, 'for itself as the expression of itself' (51). To a person who is going through an experience, it is neither tragic nor comic. To Oedipus, his plight may not have appeared tragic. Bakhtin comments, 'For the event of tragedy as an artistic performance does not coincide with the event of Oedipus's life' (52). Oedipus is a passive sufferer whereas the author is the active creator of form. In the absence of form there is no aesthetic experience. This is why Bakhtin argues that the author is 'the uniquely active form-giving energy' that is manifested in the cultural product.

The question of answerability has a bearing on the process of creation. By 'answerability', Bakhtin implies the self's need to respond to the other. Consciousness of oneself is always incomplete. In that sense, one lives in the future. Through one's actions, one projects oneself into the future. The world as a given fact has no meaning. It is through one's actions that one creates meanings. Consciousness transforms meaning. The world is shaped through value-loaded actions of individuals. Human consciousness enters the world in the form of acts that define values. Consciousnesses are not islands that exist in isolation, but are continuously connected through thoughts that relate one to the other. Our selves are constituted through these acts of interlinkages.

Confessional Self-accounting and Autobiography

Bakhtin's discussion of the author and hero with reference to certain literary forms may help us better understand his approach to the question of creativity. For instance, 'confessional self-accounting' and 'autobiography' are unique forms as the author and the hero are one and the same in these cases. As individuals, we all act through deeds, words, thoughts and feelings. We move into the future through our actions. However, our actions are not accompanied by self-reflection in the normal course. Our actions are received as part of social, political, aesthetic or ethical values. While performing a deed, a person may ask, 'what for?' or 'to what end?', and not 'who am I?' or 'what am I?' A feeling like remorse lies behind a confessional self-accounting. And this psychological state of being organises and gives form to inner life, in the confessional narrative.

In such a narrative, the relation of 'I' to itself is what is central. The other does not figure in such a relation. The self-writing is an act that does not isolate itself from the event of being. Since a person can never have the last word on himself/herself, it is potentially infinite. The question of readers' perspective towards this narrative also raises questions. Our perception of a self-accounting will inevitably tend toward aestheticising it. However, here there is no author who enables us to co-create the text. Nor is there a hero, who, together with the author can consummate it. While it defies any attempt to interpret it in terms of an author–hero relation, it may serve the function of edification, as the confessional self-accounting becomes a means of enriching oneself through spiritual experience. One gains cognisance of God through such a narrative.

Autobiography as a literary form emerged at the end of the Middle Ages, as the Renaissance ushered in a new perspective on the human subject. In Petrarch, we can see the early signs of biographical values. The penitent tone of the confessional narrative can be seen erupting into such texts. This is noticeable even in the diary form of writing. For instance, in Tolstoy's last diaries we find this tone of penance, whereas Pushkin's diaries never display such a tone. Bakhtin recognises no dividing line between autobiography and biography. 'I for myself' is not the principle of organising a biography or an autobiography. Here the author coincides with the hero. The distinctiveness of the person speaking and the person spoken of cannot be completely erased. In a biography or autobiography, the focus is on the complete life lived. In relation to that life, the author becomes the other.

There is a lot in the world that one learns about oneself from others. The world of others is an authoritative source of one's childhood, the political environment of one's childhood and forms their entire family history. What I know about myself from within myself is always fragmentary, and lacks the unity of a biography. Bakhtin comments, 'It is only an intimate, organic axiological participation in the world of others that renders the biographical self-objectification of a life authoritative and productive' (*Art and Answerability* 155). Essentially, this means that biography is a form that is rendered authentic by others. The principle of answerability is at work here. Bakhtin concludes, 'The world of biography is not a closed or definitively completed world, it is not isolated out of the unitary and unique event of being' (166). The question of knowledge and experience discussed above in the neo-Kantian context finds application here, as these concerns inform the theoretical apparatus of Bakhtin.

EVENT, EVENTNESS, EMBODIMENT

Some of these ideas are closely aligned with what Bakhtin discusses in his book, *Toward a Philosophy of the Act*. Here, Bakhtin is concerned with the 'eventness' of an act as a phenomenon that is unique in place and time. It is traceable to a subject which is embodied and situated. When we abstract an event as a general statement it loses its 'ontological roots of being' (44). As discussed earlier, Bakhtin was opposed to the 'theoreticism' that characterises much of modern knowledge, including the humanities and social sciences. These disciplines, in particular, deal with human actions which are performed by subjects rooted in place and time. It may be argued that we can escape the tendency of abstraction and objectification only by moving towards new ways of relating to human actions as in 'aesthetic seeing'.

The aestheticisation of life offers a temptation to overcome the distancing effect of theoreticism, but it does not provide a clear way out of the crisis of objectivism. The singularity of an event consists of its 'once-occurrent', non-iterative nature. Its eventness is inherent in the unique characteristics that constitute it. Aesthetic seeing is not able to enter the core area of singularity that defines an event. The reason has to be sought in the lack of answerability that aesthetic intuition suffers from. Aesthetic seeing suffers from lack of empathy, which alone can bring out the power to reach out to the other.

The larger question Bakhtin poses is: how can we access 'being-as-event'? Being is made possible through interactions, through an 'answerable consciousness'. Any act which is performed in place and time is answerable. Bakhtin writes, 'It is only from within the actually performed act, which is once occurrent, integral, and unitary in its answerability, that we can find an approach to unitary and once-occurrent being in its concrete actuality' (28). Answerability consists in taking up responsibility for one's actions, by refusing to exist as a passive subject. As a human being, one has no alibi, no excuse for not owning up to the responsibility for one's act. It is in this sense that one becomes 'answerable': 'An answerable act or deed is precisely that act which is performed on the basis of an acknowledgment of my obligative (ought-to-be) uniqueness' (42).

LANGUAGE AND EXPERIENCE

Language can capture the concrete truth of an event much more effectively than the abstract thinking about such an experience. Bakhtin explains the reason in these words: 'Historically language grew up in the service of participative thinking and performed acts, and it begins to serve abstract thinking only in the present day of its history' (*Toward a Philosophy* 31). Words as concepts and images, with their intonation, all contribute towards the unity of language. But the expressivity of language cannot always match the fullness of experience. Bakhtin holds that experiences of being-as-event are expressible, but 'full adequacy is unattainable' (31). It remains an ideal that has to be pursued. The conditions of experience in which 'the act becomes answerable of itself and is actually performed' (31) have to be described 'participatively'. It is only in such a situation that experience, meaning and history are blended into one in the unified being-as-event. This process can recover the uniqueness of things around us: tree becomes 'this tree', sky becomes 'this sky', and so on. Everything becomes relational, as the embodied subject is involved in the act as an answerable being. In the process, the world becomes humanised. The singularity of the unique human being, in this sense, makes the larger world and its diversity possible.

Once again, Bakhtin is faced with the question of the other and how as embodied subjects we relate to the other. As mentioned earlier, aesthetic seeing has limitations when it comes to overcoming the problems of theoreticism. We need to include questions of empathy within aesthetic seeing to enlarge its orbit. Bakhtin believes that aesthetic seeing should become 'participative thinking' if the former has to be addressed. 'Aesthetic contemplation' is a stage that helps us move beyond the limitations of aesthetic seeing. When we empathise, we are able to objectify the other, separate it from oneself and also return it to oneself. The various stages involved in aesthetic seeing and aesthetic contemplation lie outside the individual's consciousness. Here Bakhtin uses the term 'transgredient', which is an important term in his thought. In a note given in his book *Art and Answerability,* Bakhtin comments that Johannes Volkelt uses this term in correlation with 'trans-subjective' and continues, '"trans-subjective" is that which lies outside the sphere of my current consciousness, "transgredient" is that which lies outside the immediate being of my current act of thinking' (233). Self and cultures can complete themselves only by taking over elements from other selves and cultures. Here Bakhtin offers a critique of both classical and modern epistemology which emphasise knowing as a process involving a single consciousness. For this reason, Bakhtin emphasises the 'outsideness' of every thought. One is dependent on the other to become a true 'whole'. Empathising is an act in which we retain our individuality. It produces the other as an actual object for our individual consciousness. This object never existed before and has the power to enrich our being, being-as-event.

A Reading of Robert Lowell's 'Skunk Hour'

We shall illustrate some of the points made by Bakhtin such as 'answerability', 'artist', 'hero', 'architectonics', 'empathy' and 'participatory thinking', using the poem 'Skunk Hour' by the American poet Robert Lowell (1917–77). What makes this poem appropriate for discussing the concepts outlined above, is its central concern with 'empathy' that transforms the poet's self. The poem enacts an event that demonstrates the significance of 'answerability' as an act of taking up responsibility for one's own life. This is achieved through the poem's artistic form which involves a movement from the self to the other and back to a renewed self.

Lowell's *Life Studies* (1959) marks a breakthrough in shaping a new poetic voice by moving away from his complex modernist idiom. In the poems included in this volume, Lowell speaks of everyday experiences in a language closer to spoken language, and communicates intimate feelings of shame and humiliation in stark details. Bakhtin suggests that the unity between the individual and the artist is at the core of 'answerability'. The poet and the man or woman of everyday life have to enter into a dialogue, harmonising their separate worlds. Bakhtin says, 'I have to answer with my own life for what I have experienced and understood would not remain ineffectual in my life' (*Art and Answerability* 1).

The architectonics of the poem 'Skunk Hour' can be seen in its movement from an external landscape to an inner conflict, and a gradual evaluation of the nature of this conflict. The opening stanzas point to the decadence that has overtaken the New England society. We meet three characters from the Maine seacoast village of Castine. The hermit heiress of Nautilus island, who is 'in her dotage', buys up all the buildings facing her mansion to ensure absolute ('hierarchic') privacy for herself. Then there is the 'summer millionaire' who has fallen on evil days. The fairy decorator in the village now thinks of marriage, because there is hardly any money to be earned from his work. The village is in decline and its inhabitants face uncertain futures; nothing holds them together as a community. In his comments on the poem, Lowell remarks, 'Sterility howls through the scenery, but I try to give a tone of tolerance, humour and randomness to the sad prospect' (Parkinson 131).

The author as the speaking subject of the poem evaluates his experience as the poem moves forward. The line 'The season's ill' (54) looks within and without, as it describes the value system outside as well as the poet's own alienation. The disorientation suggested by the three rootless inhabitants of New England prefigures the isolation of the poet himself. The second part of the poem shifts towards the poet's inner world. He is in a state of mental disorientation, unable to find a way to locate himself as part of the human world. He confesses to the bleakness of his situation by referring to his voyeuristic act of 'looking for love-cars'. An earlier line in the poem, 'A red fox stain covers Blue Hill', had pointed to the sense of menace and violence that haunts the poet's world.

It is in this moment of extreme alienation that the speaking subject utters a line which is more like a piercing cry: 'My mind's not right' (54). With this line, the poem shifts to another plane. This is a moment of self-perception made possible by the inward journey of the poet's contemplative mind. He recognises the sense of malignancy that afflicts him. His mind now faces the imminent threat of dissolution. This is reflected in the lines where he declares that he himself is 'hell' (54). He feels a deep sense of disquiet that is closer to physical distress: he can hear his spirit sobbing, as if it is suffocated by his own hands. In his comments on these lines, Lowell says, 'This is the dark night. . . . My night is not gracious, but secular, puritan and agnostical. An existentialist night' (Parkinson 131–32). The line 'I myself am hell' has echoes from Marlowe's *Doctor Faustus* and Milton's *Paradise Lost.* The inter-textual resonance of this line evaluates the experience from a universal perspective, enriching the architectonics of the poem. It prepares the poem to move beyond the self, towards the other.

In the encounter with the skunks narrated in the last part of the poem, a going-forth and a return are enacted. The poet realises that he is not alone in the dark night. He is aware of a family skunks foraging the garbage for 'a bite to eat' (54). They are unaware of things other than what concern them for their survival. These animals are not burdened by questions of salvation or redemption. The oppressive sense of self-consciousness that afflicts the poet pales into insignificance in their presence. The poet's power of empathy invests this moment with an essence which his existence lacked. The artist-as-hero observes the mother skunk with her column of kittens without any revulsion. In their familial bonding and complete surrender to reality, he finds an other-centred view of the world.

In the final stanza, the poet-as-hero is face-to-face with another order of reality. The stanza presents a vision which can only come from outside one's self. The poet, while standing on the back steps, 'breathe[s] the rich air', marking a moment of reconciliation with his alienating surroundings and alienated self.

Bakhtin, while elaborating on the nature of an ethical act, remarks that it is prompted not by a mere identification with the other, but 'a return to myself, a *return* to my own place outside the suffering person' (*Art and Answerability* 26; emphasis as in the original). Ethical behaviour demands a certain distance from the other, 'a distance which for Bakhtin is the precondition of human concern and love' (Hirschkop 70). In the architectonics of the poem, the encounter with the skunks is a 'once-occurrent act' that enables the poet-as-hero to discover the nature of his inner conflict. In empathising with the lowest of the low, the hero strikes a chord with the world outside. It is an ethical act of answerability where he apprehends the self–other relation in their interdependent unity. The self is renewed and it returns to the artist as a gift from the other. According to Bakhtin, 'confessional self-accounting is filled with the need for forgiveness and redemption as an absolutely *pure gift* (an unmerited gift), with the need for a mercy and grace that are totally otherworldly in respect to their value' (*Art and Answerability* 143). The poet could notice the vitality and tenacity of the skunks because he desperately needed an affirmative sign from the outer world. We are reminded of a similar scene from Coleridge's 'The Rime of the Ancient Mariner' where the sight of the water-snakes transforms the bleak reality of the mariner's despair into a moment of vision. Lowell's encounter with the skunks helps him overcome a suicidal moment of extreme despair. From an 'aesthetic contemplation' he moves to 'participative thinking', through a moment of recognition and reconciliation.

UNFINALISABILITY

It is also important to understand what Bakhtin means by 'finalisation' and 'unfinalisability'. Many terms that figure in the above discussion, such as 'valuation', 'surplus of vision' and 'outsidedness', all point to certain core concepts in Bakhtin's thought. 'Valuation' suggests that all understanding involves a real exchange of values. An utterance is specific historically because it carries a social evaluation. Similarly, one achieves self-knowledge only by moving beyond the limits of one's own self. If we ground meaning and understanding in 'theoretical being', we find ourselves 'determined, predetermined, bygone and finished, essentially not living' (*Toward a Philosophy* 9). Such a perspective is rooted in theoreticism, which ignores the contingent elements that constitute human reality. Such a limiting way of essentialising the human world renders it finalisable whereas Bakhtin conceives human beings in terms of 'living historicity' (8). For Bakhtin, human beings exist meaningfully only when they are open and unfinalisable. The axiomatic openness is a precondition to understand the eventness of once-occurrent being. Being can never be conceived in terms of a closed, finished event. Bakhtin comments, 'In order to live and act, I need to be unfinalized. I need to be open for myself . . . I have to be, for myself, someone, who is axiologically yet-to-be, someone who does not coincide with his already existing makeup' (*Art and Answerability* 13).

As an open, unfinalisable living subject one is constantly oriented towards a future which is yet-to-be. It is one's answerability which constitutes openness towards the other. As long as one is open to the other, and is formed by the other, they will not be finalised or finished. It is the dialogic communication that sustains life and makes us living subjects. As a continuously evolving subject, one can become other than what one is now. This is possible due to one's openness to the other. 'Architectonics' is the term Bakhtin uses to describe his analytical framework, which is not a theoretical structure with closed constituents, but a formulation which emphasises the eventness of being, its historicity and unfinalisability, and the incompleteness of living things. Bakhtin's ideas on language and literature must be approached from this perspective.

It has been pointed out that the Bakhtin circle also had some Indologists who were familiar with Buddhist philosophy and logic. There was a marked difference in the way Orientalism developed in many of the European countries ('From Indo-European Philology' 21–33). British Indology was complicit in perpetuating imperialism and developed arguments that justified European superiority over the people of Asia. Germany was one of the countries where language and race came to be aligned in the study of the past. Friedrich Max Müller was a German philologist who taught Sanskrit at Oxford University and was actively involved in the propagation of classical Sanskrit texts. He did not anticipate that this would go on to pave the way for a theory of Indo-Aryan supremacy. A critique of this tendency developed in Russia in the 1920s, particularly in the wake of the October Revolution of 1917. The Bakhtin circle included scholars like Nikolai Iosifovich Konrad, who specialised in Japanese and Chinese literature, and Mikhail Izrailovich Tubianskii, an Indologist (27). Brandist, in his article on the relations between the Bakhtin circle and Indology, comments,

> The "dialogic" structure of Indian philosophical discourse was something the school insisted upon, holding that it was impossible to examine one system without studying all the others since the propositions of each of the systems contained responses to the alternative views of its opponents, which were at once taken into account, assimilated and often even appropriated. (27)

A well-known Russian Sanskritologist, Fedor Shcherbatskoi (also spelt as Theodor Stcherbatsky), published a two-volume work titled *Buddhist Logic* in 1930–32. Otto Rosenberg, who was his student, published *Buddhist Philosophy* in 1919. Tubianskii translated the poetry and prose of Tagore in the 1920s. All this is ample evidence to suggest that Bakhtin was sufficiently informed about Indian philosophical traditions, and that this must have contributed to the development of his arguments outlined above, which attempt to overcome the abstract logicism of neo-Kantian philosophy. The important point to note is that Bakhtin's ideas attempt to overcome 'the ethno-centrism of contemporary European philology' (33). Brandist concludes, 'Thus, Bakhtin's work on the novel emerges from a specific intellectual environment in which attempts to overcome the ideological dichotomy between East and West played an important role' (33).

UTTERANCES

Utterances, as explained above, are context-bound. In daily life, different situations demand a large variety of speech types. A speaker chooses appropriate sounds, words, intonation and syntax in verbalising his/her intention or thoughts. Each sphere of communication has its unique thematic, stylistic and compositional structure of language. A lawyer's use of language will differ from that of a doctor. Neither of them will share much in common with a mason's use of language. Bakhtin observes, 'Each separate utterance is individual, of course, but each sphere in which language is used develops its own *relatively stable types* of these utterances. These we may call *speech genres*' (Morris 81). In any given society, human activities remain endless and hence speech genres are infinite. A priest's sermon, a military officer's command, a business letter, a judge's verdict, a news broadcast, or people speaking at a bus stop: it is this inexhaustible list of human situations that accounts for the endless variety of speech genres. Bakhtin comments, 'If speech genres did not exist and we had not mastered them, if we had to originate them during the speech process and construct each utterance at will for the first time, speech communication would be almost impossible' (84).

When we learn a language, we learn how to make utterances and this involves the use of speech genres. Molière's character, Monsieur Jourdain was surprised to discover that he had been speaking prose all his life. According to Bakhtin, we speak in diverse genres without knowing that they exist. Speech situations fall into certain patterns and what we internalise is the appropriate utterance that is demanded by a particular speech situation. The speaker's evaluation of what he/she is talking about also becomes part of his/her speech. This is what makes his/her speech unique. When someone begins to speak in response to our utterance, we form a sense of the whole at the very beginning. The speech genre alerts us to the forthcoming speech as a whole at the very beginning. One's evaluation of what one is talking about also enters one's speech. This is conveyed by choice of words, style of communication and the speech genre used. It is this evaluative aspect of one's speech that makes it personal and unique. This is where our freedom manifests as the expressive function of an utterance. While most speech exchanges in daily life, like an enquiry at the counter of a bus station, are 'codified' and have no 'expressive' component, informal and intimate conversations are rich in expressive content as they are unpredictable and are not subjected to 'generic' control. The expressive quality of individual words cannot be traced to the words themselves. Bakhtin argues that it is the 'generic expression' or 'the echo of another's individual expression' (85) that accounts for their expressiveness.

Bakhtin makes a distinction between simple and complex speech genres. A conversation between two speakers is an example of a simple speech genre. However, a novel, play, short story or a scientific treatise is an example of a complex speech genre. A complex speech genre is made up of many simple speech genres, and in the process of their assimilation into higher complex genres, the constituent primary genres get modified. The novel is a complex utterance which reflects the heteroglossia of society. The complex plurality of speech genres in the social sphere is what creates heteroglossia, which has already been mentioned before and will be elaborated on further in the next chapter.

Utterances also form a network, each of them being a response to a previous one, while anticipating another utterance in turn. Traces of others' utterances will be present in our utterances, sometimes as a direct reference, as a quote, or as an interpretation or reinterpretation. Sometimes, the other utterance may be a presence in the speech chain, as an assumption known to all. Knowing the thematic content of an utterance is not enough to understand the full meaning of one's utterance. Bakhtin writes, 'The expression of an utterance always *responds* to a greater or lesser degree, that is, it expresses the speaker's attitude towards others' utterances and not just his attitude towards the object of his utterance' (86). We speak in response to someone else's speech. Expressiveness is a matter of responding to the other. Even in the most monologic kinds of utterances, like a scientific tract, there will be traces of others' utterances in its composition and style. Bakhtin makes it clear that all our thoughts are formed in the context of others' thoughts and ideas. It is in the process of interaction that ideas get their shape and moral clarity.

According to Bakhtin, the quality of an utterance being directed at someone may be referred to as 'addressivity'. The speaker's perception of the addressee is what shapes the utterance in a certain way. The choice of speech genres in the course of an utterance is dictated by the addressee. The addressee may be someone present before you, or a community of experts for whom you are composing the utterance, a large public gathering, your followers, disciples or opponents. Bakhtin concludes, 'Each speech genre in each area of speech communication has its own typical conception of the addressee, and this defines it as a genre' (87).

BAKHTIN'S RELATION WITH POSTSTRUCTURALISM

Some of the basic postulations of poststructuralist thought follow from the neo-Kantian approach to questions of language and experience. This is what makes Bakhtin closer to the poststructuralist worldview. The idea that language constitutes the world for us is primary in the approaches of Bakhtin and the poststructuralists. Foucault would argue that the object of knowledge is discursively constituted. The empirical world can only be known as part of the signified, but this objective world is being continuously formed, and is never present as an object. Cassirer's idea of 'symbolic forms' posits how the human consciousness conceptualises reality as it evolves from different perspectives. The human capacity for evolving symbolic forms is foundational to the creativity of human society. Cassirer observes that the living process of speech is one in which 'individuality and universality are contained as equally justified and equally necessary aspects of the process' (16). Echoes of this approach can be found in Bakhtin's view of utterance. Cassirer further explains that 'the universal is that through which the individual constructs the world, and the universal is what constructs the world of the individual' (16–17).

For Bakhtin, the utterance partakes of the innermost individualistic traits even as it becomes part of a larger universal communicative process.

EXPERIENCE AND EXPRESSION

One of Bakhtin's key insights is that culture is a contested field where competing ideological forces are constantly engaged in a struggle to establish dominance. The centripetal and centrifugal forces inform and shape the language of expression which, in turn, shapes experience. In contemporary times, the question of experience and expression has been the subject of many discussions. In *Cracked Mirror* (2013) Gopal Guru and Sundar Sarukkai debate these issues but they seem to be unaware that Bakhtin has discussed these questions threadbare from a philosophical viewpoint much earlier. Bakhtin's objection to theoreticism was based on its inability to recognise the eventness of once-occurrent experience. Sundar Sarukkai's argument echoes Bakhtin: 'Lived experience should be seen as the experience of being a subject and not an experience by a subject about a subject' (37). 'Being a subject' is a dynamic state which is continuously shaped from within and without. This is why a theoretical formulation is unable to grasp it in its entirety without falsifying it. Theory which is purely empirical negates experience. When experience becomes a universal category, without reference to a subject rooted in a culturally specific time and place, it loses its ideological relevance. This points to a larger ethical question which lies at the heart of Bakhtin's theory of answerability, outsidedness and addressivity. A social and political thinker like Dr Babasaheb Ambedkar also realised the importance of being engaged in meaningful communication across social divisions like caste, to create a modern secular society. He observes,

> And the only way in which men can come to possess things in common with one another is by being in communication with one another. This is merely another way of saying that society continues to exist by communication. To make things concrete, it is not enough if men act in a way which agrees with the acts of others. Parallel activity is not sufficient to bind men into a society. (Ambedkar 269)

It is important to recognise that people become part of a community only when they share social spaces and their discourses intermingle. The caste system prevented boundaries from becoming porous and open. It also stopped discourses from penetrating each other. Bakhtin's emphasis is on ethical living. The larger question Ambedkar also raises is how can one exist as an ethical being in a divided society?

One of the primary concerns of ethics, is our relation with the other. Words in the social context are accented with the desires, intentions, attitudes, assumptions, preferences and prejudices circulating in a speech community. This is where ethics becomes the defining aspect of a living society's linguistic resources. It is dissenting speech that breaches the self-sufficiency of a hegemonic power structure. An act of dissent is a critical act, opening up the social space in which it is performed. It uses a mode that both interrogates and exceeds its immediate purpose. It draws attention to the very manner in which it is spoken.

REFERENCES

Ambedkar, B. R. *The Essential Writings of B. R. Ambedkar*. Ed. Valerian Rodrigues. New Delhi: Oxford UP, 2002. Print.

Bakhtin, Mikhail M. *Art and Answerability: Early Philosophical Essays*. Ed. Michael Holquist and Vadim Liapunov. Trans. Vadim Liapunov. Austin: U of Texas P, 1990. Print.

---. *Toward a Philosophy of the Act*. Trans. Vadim Liapunov. Ed. Vadim Liapunov and Michael Holquist. Austin: U of Texas P, 1993. Print.

Brandist, Craig. 'From Indo-European Philology to the Bakhtin Circle.' *Bakhtinian Explorations of Indian Culture: Pluralism, Dogma and Dialogue through History*. Ed. Lakshmi Bandlamudi and E. V. Ramakrishnan. New Delhi: Springer, 2018. Print.

Cassirer, Ernst. *The Metaphysics of Symbolic Forms*. New Haven: Yale UP, 1954. Print. Vol. 4. of *The Philosophy of Symbolic Forms*.

Clark, Katerina, and Michael Holquist. *Mikhail Bakhtin*. Cambridge, MA: The Belknap Press (Harvard UP), 1984. Print.

Guru, Gopal, and Sundar Sarukkai. *The Cracked Mirror: An Indian Debate on Experience and Theory*. New Delhi: Oxford UP, 2013. Print.

Hirschkop, Ken. *The Cambridge Introduction to Mikhail Bakhtin*. Cambridge: Cambridge UP, 2021. Print.

Lowell, Robert. 'Skunk Hour'. *Selected Poems*. London: Faber and Faber, 1965. Print.

Morris, Pam, ed. *The Bakhtin Reader: Selected Writings of Bakhtin, Medvedev, Voloshinov*. London: Arnold Publishers, 1994. Print.

Parkinson, Thomas, ed. *Robert Lowell: A Collection of Critical Essays*. Twentieth Century Views. New Jersey: Prentice Hall, 1968. Print. (The discussion of 'Skunk Hour' by Robert Lowell is on pages 131–33.)

Steinby, Liisa. 'Hermann Cohen and Bakhtin's Early Aesthetics.' *Studies in East European Thought* 63.3 (August, 2011): 227–49. Print.

Chapter Four

Dostoevsky's Polyphonic Novel

CONCEPTS AND CATEGORIES

One of Bakhtin's greatest contributions to literary criticism is embodied in his book-length study on the novels of Fyodor Dostoevsky. Bakhtin worked on this study in the 1920s, and published *The Problems of Dostoevsky's Art* in 1929. The work was received well, even earning a favourable review from a Bolshevik critic who was a Minister of Education. However, this did not prevent Bakhtin's arrest the same year by the communist government. The book was republished under the title *Problems of Dostoevsky's Poetics* in 1963, when a new generation of readers rediscovered Bakhtin and sought him out in his reclusive isolation in Saransk. He agreed to revise the book at their request, hence the present work we have on Dostoevsky's poetics is the revised edition. The book went through four more editions during Bakhtin's lifetime. It was translated into English by Caryl Emerson in 1984 and was published by the University of Minnesota Press.

Through his analysis of Dostoevsky's novels, Bakhtin found a new vocabulary to talk about the novel as a genre. As Wayne Booth suggests in his introduction to the book, the conventions of criticism of the novel as a genre were overturned by Bakhtin. For him, the artist's essential task is 'to achieve a view of the world superior to all other views; fiction of the right kind, pursuing the right tasks, is the best instrument of understanding that has ever been devised' (*Problems of* xx). The novelistic form is the only way to understand and represent the essential multi-centredness or polyphony of human life. The novel as a form is unlike other literary forms, as it has the potential to realise the multi-voiced quality of lives lived among others. While genres tend to bestow a level of coherence on the work of art, resisting the inherent plurality suggested by experiences, the novel as a genre has the potential to embody points of view of characters which are unlike those of the authors. According to Bakhtin, Dostoevsky's novels realise this potential to the maximum.

Several critics have noted that Dostoevsky's characters such as Raskolnikov, Ivan Karamazov, Stavrogin and the Grand Inquisitor are independent of their author in their fictional worlds. The reader can enter into conversations with these characters and be part of the dialogues in the novels. In order to explain this quality of Dostoevsky's novelistic discourse, Bakhtin uses the term 'polyphonic novel': 'A plurality of independent and unmerged voices and consciousnesses, a genuine polyphony of fully valid voices is in fact the chief characteristic of Dostoevsky's novels' (6). The narrative of a Dostoevskian novel does not reflect a single objective world with a single authorial consciousness. His heroes are 'subjects of their own directly signifying discourse' (7). The hero does not act as a medium to objectify the author's point of view; instead, the hero has his own point of view just like the author: 'In his works a hero appears whose voice is constructed exactly like the voice of the author himself in a novel of the usual type' (7).

Often the fictional world of Dostoevsky appears chaotic. This is because we use the same criteria to evaluate them as we do for monologic novels. Dostoevsky's works must be evaluated on the basis of his dialogic vision. Critics tend to view these novels through the lens of philosophical or psychological concepts. Their focus is usually on the themes of the novels. But according to Bakhtin, one cannot understand Dostoevsky unless one grasps the peculiar dialogic nature of the architectonics of his novels.

Dostoevsky's novels are profoundly personal. The thoughts and ideas embodied in his novels are represented through the consciousness of a living person who belongs to a specific time and place. Critics have attempted to describe the phenomenon through various critical strategies but have failed to fully represent the breakthrough achieved by Dostoevsky in fictional representation. In Dostoevsky, the narrative is not oriented towards objectifying the characters, but representing them as autonomous subjects. However, critics who are unable to understand this process, have described the independent consciousnesses of characters as 'objectified things', reducing Dostoevsky's fictional world to monologic terms. They have failed to grasp the unique architectonics of Dostoevsky's fictional world.

DOSTOEVSKY'S RUSSIAN CRITICS

Dostoevsky looks at the world through the personalised views of his characters. It is through the living voice of an integral person that the world of ideas and thoughts comes alive in his works. Bakhtin discusses Dostoevsky's major critics in Russian literature, such as Vyacheslav Ivanov, Sergei Askoldov, Leonid Grossman and Otto Kaus. Each of them locates the unique significance of his narrative art and philosophical vision in a different set of principles which are unable to account for his architectonic singularity. Grossman, for instance, notes how Dostoevsky's novels go against the grain of the canonical European novel in not shaping the diverse aspects of the narrative into an organic unity with a unified and integral artistic creation. He mentions that 'the Book of Job, the Revelation of St. John, the Gospel texts . . . everything that feeds the pages of his novels . . . is combined here in a most original way with the newspaper, the anecdote, the parody, the street scene, with the grotesque, even with the pamphlet' (qtd. in *Problems of* 15).

Grossman, thus, is able to bring out the narrative uniqueness of Dostoevsky graphically, but concludes that his highly heterogenous material takes on 'the deep imprint of his personal style and tone' (qtd. in *Problems of* 15). What he fails to comprehend is that Dostoevsky's heterogeneity is not subjected or subordinated to the unity of a personal style. His novels are not pervaded by the presence of an overpowering single consciousness. Dostoevsky's novels do not carry the signature of the author's singular style. They carry many styles, are multi-accented and project values that are contradictory. An all-pervasive, homogenous unity of vision does not envelope all the heterogenous material in his novels. These diverse materials belong to multiple worlds and separate autonomous consciousnesses which exist in their varied fields of vision. The polyphonic novel is characterised by the existence of such parallel worlds which are autonomous in themselves.

Grossman had also pointed out the importance of dialogues in Dostoevsky's novels and traced it to the author's allegiance to multiple ideologies. Bakhtin feels that Grossman failed to relate the artistic design of Dostoevsky's novels, which he correctly identified, to the plurality of points of view clashing within the novels. In other words, he was not able to identity these elements as defining features of a polyphonic vision.

Bakhtin draws attention to the basic differences between drama and the novel. Dialogues in a drama do not destabilise the unity of the represented 'monolithic world' of the plot. Bakhtin writes, 'The rejoinders in a dramatic dialogue do not rip apart the represented world, do not make it multi-leveled; on the contrary, if they are to be authentically dramatic, these rejoinders necessitate the utmost monolithic unity of that world' (*Problems of* 17). Drama succeeds only if the monolithic quality of its world is maintained. There is a single, unified field of vision which the characters inhabit. If there are multiple levels of consciousnesses and action in a play, the idea of dramatic action that resolves contradictions cannot be sustained. It is important to understand Bakhtin's view that in Dostoevsky's novels, there is 'no non-participating third person' (18).

Otto Kaus shows how Dostoevsky's novels are replete with 'utterly contradictory and mutually exclusive concepts, judgements and evaluations' (18). Each one of them is validated by the narrative. Kaus argues that these disparate worlds were self-contained wholes with their own autonomous existence before the advent of capitalism. Capitalism destroyed their exclusive nature and ideological self-sufficiency. Bakhtin agrees with Kaus's argument and comments that unlike elsewhere in Europe where capitalism advanced gradually, in Russia it 'catastrophically' came upon a large number of multiple disparate worlds (20), with disruptive consequences. A meditative monologic consciousness could not have contained their contradictions within its framework. However, Kaus is unable to explore the multi-voiced novelistic narrative of Dostoevsky further. It is to his credit that he does not try to unify and homogenise the contradictions contained in the narrative of Dostoevsky's novels.

B. M. Engelhardt's essay 'Dostoevsky's Ideological Novel' shows how Dostoevsky's heroes are embodiments of ideas. This makes his novels ideological. Ideas have independent life in the Dostoevskian hero's consciousness. Bakhtin argues that in Dostoevsky's novels there is no evolution of any single, central idea. Through his 'profoundly *pluralistic*' (26) world, he presents the interconnectedness of ideas.

IDEAS AND IDEOLOGIES IN DOSTOEVSKY

Bakhtin believes that the times in which Dostoevsky lived made the existence of the polyphonic world in his novels possible. He believed in several ideologies at different points in his life, which helped him represent them authentically. They were part of the contradictions of the period he lived in. Bakhtin comments, 'The fundamental category in Dostoevsky's mode of artistic visualizing was not evolution, but *coexistence* and *interaction*' (28). While a writer like Goethe tends to view all contradictions as part of an evolving sequence, Dostoevsky juxtaposes them in their interrelationships. He tends to see everything in the world in their simultaneity. This explains why Dostoevsky uses doubles in his novels. The contradiction within a character is dramatised using the device of doubles. This also extends to his use of crowd scenes, where a single moment holds the largest diversity. Actions take place quickly in his novels as the narrative triumphs over time. His interest in the characters extends only to the extent of their relationships to one another. He is not interested in their individual biographies. Only those events pertaining to each character which have a bearing on the ongoing action are narrated by Dostoevsky. Bakhtin concludes, 'Dostoevsky portrayed not the life of an idea in an isolated consciousness, and not the interrelationship of ideas, but the interaction of consciousnesses in the sphere of ideas (but not of ideas only)' (32).

The views of A. V. Lunacharsky outlined in his essay 'On Dostoevsky's "Multi-voicedness"' are closer to some of Bakhtin's own views. He argues that 'Dostoevsky's novels are in fact brilliantly staged dialogues' (qtd. in *Problems of* 33). Lunacharsky also traces the lineage of the idea of polyphony in European literature and finds Shakespeare one of the most important practitioners of polyphony. Bakhtin is not fully in agreement with this point of view, as he believes drama as a genre is essentially monologic. According to Bakhtin, the works of writers such as Rabelais and Cervantes serve as better examples of polyphony. Lunacharsky examines in great detail the nature of Dostoevsky's epoch and concludes that it was the contradictions of the period that infused Dostoevsky's works with its essential multi-voicedness.

Bakhtin finds that the criticism of Dostoevsky's novels in the 1930s and 40s did not produce any major work. He does mention V. Kirpotin, whose comment, 'Dostoevsky had the capacity to visualize directly someone else's psyche' (qtd. in *Problems of* 36) is cited as an example of his insightful analysis. Bakhtin adds that Kirpotin fails to see that Dostoevsky's psychologism is not individual-centric, but social. Another critic he approvingly quotes is Grossman, whose later critical work explores the musical quality of Dostoevsky's novels. This detailed analysis of Dostoevsky's criticism leads Bakhtin to conclude that, by and large, critics have focused on the ideologies of Dostoevsky's heroes. In the process, they have 'monologised' his novels by failing to see his uniqueness in deliberately not creating a unified field of vision.

THE HERO AND AUTHOR IN DOSTOEVSKY'S NOVELS

Some of these ideas are further elaborated by Bakhtin in his chapter on 'The Hero, and the Position of the Author with Regard to the Hero, in Dostoevsky's Art'. The polyphonic novel is characterised by the freedom and independence enjoyed by the hero and his/her voice in the structure of the novel. The hero, for Dostoevsky, is not a character to manipulate according to his imaginary whims. He is a 'particular point of view on the world and on himself' (47). What Dostoevsky describes is not the external reality from the hero's perspective, but the significance of this external world for the hero. Bakhtin believes that Dostoevsky brought about a Copernican revolution in the creation of novelistic discourse. The author is now reconstituted as an aspect of the hero's self-definition. Bakhtin observes that in Dostoevsky's works the hero's 'voice is constructed in the same way as is the author's own voice in the usual type of novel' (7). The character's word about himself and about his world is accorded as much importance as the author's word and 'is not subordinated to the objectified image of character, as one of his characteristics, nor does it serve as the mouth-piece of authorial voice' (7).

The Dostoevskian hero's entire life is concentrated on the process of gaining consciousness of himself and the world. His characters like the Dreamer or the Underground Man are not personified as individuals. Their self-consciousness becomes the artistic dominant in the novelistic world. Usually when the hero becomes the mouthpiece of the author, they become inseparable from each other. Such a fusion does not take place in Dostoevsky's novels. Here, the hero has a separate existence and whatever we know of the hero is also known to the hero himself/herself. The Underground Man is aware of the most minute details of his internal and external traits. The author is not the privileged source of rare information about the hero. In a monologic novel, 'the hero is closed and his semantic boundaries are clearly defined' (51). The consciousness of the Underground Man is characterised by its 'unfinalizability, unclosedness and indeterminacy' (53). In the scheme of things in Dostoevsky's world, the hero is not an objectified image, but an autonomous discourse. We can hear him through his voice in his discourse. This kind of narration also imparts a touch of fantasy to the Dostoevskian novel. This is because the hero's point of view has to incorporate another field of vision in its entirety. In realistic fiction, we often find the author commenting on the hero, turning him/her into a voiceless object. This denies the hero any self-consciousness of his/her own. The Dostoevskian hero does not emerge as a finalised person as seen through the author's perspective. Bakhtin writes, 'The author of a polyphonic novel is not required to renounce himself or his own consciousness, but he must to an extraordinary extent broaden, deepen and rearrange this consciousness . . . in order to accommodate the autonomous consciousnesses of others' (68).

Dostoevsky rarely depicts the death of his heroes. This is because his interest lies in their consciousness as it develops and interacts with the world around it. Any truth that is communicated to the reader is introduced in 'the dialogic field of vision of all the other major heroes of the novel' (73).

Dostoevsky, as an author, never retains any surplus of meaning which is not accessible to his heroes. He only retains the minimum surplus of information which is required to take the story forward. Bakhtin's following comments on Raskolnikov help us understand Bakhtin's central argument: 'All possible evaluations and points of view on his personality, his character, his idea, his acts are extended to his own consciousness and addressed to him in dialogues with Porfiry, Sonya, Svidrigailov, Dounia, and others. All others' perception of the world intersects with his perception. . . .' (75). The author retains for himself no essential 'surplus' of meaning and enters on an equal footing with Raskolnikov into the great dialogue of the novel as a whole.

In a typical monologic novel, the author's idea overpowers all principles of representation. In such a work of art, idea is either affirmed or repudiated. It cannot create an autonomous consciousness in relation with other ideas. In the Dostoevskian novel, the hero's discourse about himself/herself along with his/her ideological discourse about the world increases the signifying power of the narrative. Bakhtin argues that monologism found its most extensive expression in idealistic philosophy. In such a philosophy a single idea regulates all worldviews. Such a monistic principle denies plurality of views and demands unity of consciousness. It was during the European Enlightenment that rationalism attained the status of such a monistic ideology controlling all expressions of consciousness. It gave rise to the cult of unified and exclusive reason.

In the ideological world of the monological novel, the ideas of the author carry the stamp of authority. They become the principle for visualising and representing the world. The world of the novel becomes an illustration of an idea. The author's ideas and the hero's ideological position coincide in the very structure of the narrative. There may be works of art where the hero exceeds the demands of a particular plot, as in some works belonging to the Romantic period. In some works, the author's ideas may get scattered as sayings, maxims and arguments which are not identified with any particular character. What distinguishes Dostoevsky is that he is able to represent someone else's idea, without assimilating it into his point of view and without violating its sanctity.

Dostoevsky's characters are caught in the turmoil of conflicting thoughts. Characters such as Raskolnikov, Ivan Karamazov and Alyosha are constantly engaged in discussions on questions related to religion and spirituality. They are seized of higher matters, subjects beyond the mundane. This also makes them unselfish. Sonya and Ivan, even Raskolnikov who commits a murder, are examples of this selflessness. Dostoevsky knew that an idea cannot be traced to a single consciousness. Only when an idea enters into a dialogic relationship with other ideas, will it develop and generate other ideas. Ideas flourish when consciousnesses interact and communicate. Bakhtin writes that an idea, just like a word, wants to be 'heard, understood, and "answered" by other voices from other positions' (88). Similarly, just as the word, the idea is dialogic in nature, and monologue functions merely as the 'conventional compositional form of its expression, a form that emerged out of the ideological monologism of modern times characterized by us above' (88).

Raskolnikov's ideas are echoed in other characters as they question and respond to him. Ivan Karamazov's argument that 'everything is permitted if there is no immortality of the soul' (Dostoevsky 81) reverberates through the entire novel through heterogenous situations and contexts.

Dostoevsky was convinced that ideas had their prototypes in the past and would assume new shapes in future. Bakhtin quotes a statement from Dostoevsky to drive home his philosophical disposition: 'Reality in its entirety is not to be exhausted by what is immediately at hand, for an overwhelming part of this reality is contained in the form of a still *latent, unuttered future Word*' (*Problems of* 90). For Dostoevsky, the thought or idea is integrally related to the individual consciousness of which it is a part. For him, an idea has to be personified in an individual. Each person becomes a point of view. Even in his journalistic articles, Dostoevsky uses voices and points of view to depict ideas interacting with each other, and he does not prioritise one at the cost of the other. Bakhtin discusses one of Dostoevsky's articles, 'The Environment', in some detail. He illustrates Dostoevsky's manner of developing a thought through the juxtaposition of a profoundly individualised voice. Everywhere he hears voices in their specific, individual contexts. This is what enabled Dostoevsky to hear 'his epoch as a great dialogue, to detect in it not just separate voices, but above all *dialogic relations* between voices, their dialogic interaction' (90). In each of his novels, a single dominant idea is closely explored to its logical conclusion through discussions, arguments and interrogations from multiple perspectives, all of which constitute a multiplicity of *voices* oriented towards the other.

CHARACTERISTICS OF THE NOVELISTIC GENRE

In the fourth chapter of his work on Dostoevsky, 'Characteristics of Genre and Plot Composition in Dostoevsky's Works', Bakhtin takes up issues related to genres and narrative structures in the polyphonic novel. In most of the types of novels belonging to the nineteenth century, such as the biographical novel, socio-psychological novel, novel of everyday life or family novel, polyphony is not a dominant feature. Bakhtin argues that Dostoevsky's polyphonic novel has to be traced to the European tradition of the adventure novel. This has been discussed by Grossman who comments that 'there is not a single attribute of the old novel of adventure which Dostoevsky failed to use' (qtd. in *Problems of* 102). The adventure plot, besides retaining the interest of the reader, cultivates 'a spark of sympathy for the insulted and the injured' (qtd. in *Problems of* 102). Since unpredictability is a feature of the adventure novel, the extra-ordinary can enter into the world of the ordinary.

Bakhtin, however, feels that these features are peripheral to Dostoevsky's novels. The humanness of the heroes of the family novel, everyday novel or biographical novel are completely enclosed and finalised in their concrete specificity. There is no contingency left. This is not true of the adventure plot. The hero of the adventure novel is propelled by his/her 'eternal human nature' which consists in 'self-preservation, the thirst for victory and triumph, the thirst for dominance or for sensual love' (105). The plot offers Dostoevsky the freedom to realise his artistic design. His polyphonic interpretation of a traditional genre opened up new possibilities in the genre of the novel.

Bakhtin argues that behind every contemporary genre, there are older forms of literature: 'A genre lives in the present, but always *remembers* its past, its beginning. Genre is a representative of creative memory in the process of literary development' (106). In the history of genres, serio-comic genres like Socratic dialogues with their 'folk-carnivalistic roots' (110, 132), and Menippean satires with carnivalisation permeating its 'external layers and deepest core' (133), are fundamentally different from serious genres such as the epic, tragedy, history and classical rhetoric. They are not concerned with the mythical past as in the epic or tragedy, but with the *living present.* They rely on experience and free invention, and they are multi-voiced.

Dostoevsky's novels are about human relations in their continuous process of becoming. For this reason, he hardly pays any attention to the world of nature, the external features of the scene being narrated or the everyday world of objects. Bakhtin observes, 'In Dostoevsky there is no objective representation of the environment, of everyday life, of nature, of objects, that is, no representation of all those things that could become a support for the author' (99). These external scenes are presented as part of the characters' way of apprehending the world. The author only comes into contact with characters as they interact and evolve through a dialogic understanding of the world.

SOCRATIC DIALOGUES AND MENIPPEAN SATIRES

As mentioned earlier, Bakhtin argues that novelistic genres have their roots in antiquity in various forms such as Socratic dialogues and Menippean satires. Socratic dialogues grew out of a folk–carnivalistic base, and project a carnivalistic view of the world. At the heart of the Socratic dialogues is the dialogic sense of truth. It is rooted in the belief that no one has complete monopoly over truth, and that it is born in the process of a collective search, a dialogic interaction. Socratic dialogues use the strategies of juxtaposition of multiple points of view, or consistently probing the other for clarification of their perspectives. Socrates was known for the latter method of provocative questioning in order to arrive at a better understanding of people's perspectives. Socratic dialogues test the claims of truth through extended conversations. Every participant in a Socratic dialogue becomes an ideologist participating in a search for truth. There is a plot situation in the dialogue which enables the mode of questioning and speaking as in Plato's *Apology*. The Socratic dialogue did not survive in history but in the course of its disintegration, it gave rise to other dialogic genres including the Menippean satires. Their roots go back to carnivalised folklore.

Menippus of Gadara (third century BCE) perfected satire into a classical form. From Antisthenes, a disciple of Socrates, to Seneca, one can trace a separate history of this genre. It was prevalent in the Middle Ages, the Renaissance and Reformation, and survived into the nineteenth century. It is not restrained by any demand of external realism. The use of fantasy allows this genre to seek truth in the most diverse situations. The fantastic takes on the character of an adventure story. The focus is on the testing of an idea, a truth, not the exploration of individual character. Often in Menippean satires, the adventures of truth also involve realism of the kind where the vulgar is incorporated into the narrative. As Bakhtin writes, 'the idea here fears no slum, is not afraid of any of life's filth' (*Problems of* 115). Its ability to pose universal questions which have philosophical implications is what makes it unique. The plot moves between Olympus, the nether world, and the mortal realm, embracing all three worlds.

This tradition, with some differences, continues in Rabelais, Swift and Voltaire. In Menippean satire, for the first time, we witness moral–psychological experimentation: 'a representation of the unusual, abnormal moral and psychic states of man—insanity of all sorts (the theme of the maniac), split personality, unrestrained daydreaming, unusual dreams, passions bordering on madness, suicides, and so forth' (116).

These are situations when the possibilities of another person and another life are revealed within one person. The dialogic relation with one's own life takes on the shape of a double. The situation can be both tragic and comic. Often in Dostoevsky, the use of doubles entails such a tragicomic situation. This kind of literature also includes utopian elements. It may manifest itself as dreams or long journeys. This genre often allows for the insertion of elements from other genres such as novellas, letters, oratorical speeches and symposia. This also helps to make it polyphonic and multi-voiced. Bakhtin concludes that one can find all the defining features of Menippean satires, with appropriate modifications and complications, in the works of Dostoevsky. It was not his subjective memory, but the objective memory of the very genre in which he worked that brought into play the above-mentioned features in his works.

Bakhtin goes on to discuss the nature of the carnival and carnivalisation of literature. These have not been outlined here as they will be taken up for detailed discussion in a separate chapter. Bakhtin demonstrates the folk–carnival base of Socratic dialogues. They were aimed at setting thought and imagination free, without surrendering to false notions of singleness of things. The joyful relativity of all things was celebrated in such performances. Similarly, carnivalisation penetrates the deepest layers of Menippean satires. The plot moves between multiple worlds. What makes these genres different is their ability to pose ultimate questions on life and death, 'a universalism of the most extreme sort (personal problems and elaborate philosophical argumentation are unknown to it)' (134).

Bakhtin illustrates how these features of carnivalisation function in the plot compositions in Dostoevsky's fiction. He singles out for detailed analysis two stories, 'Bobok' (1873), and 'The Dream of a Ridiculous Man' (1877), and some of his major novels. In the former, the narrator is on the threshold of insanity and visits a burial ground where he witnesses several burials and also listens to the conversations between buried people. Such a setting allows the author to raise questions of life and death, life after death, consciousness of death and in death, and so on. Bakhtin argues that the carnival square, which was the setting for public performances of carnivals, is recreated in these novels through the enactment of a central event in a space which takes on elements of a public place. For instance, in his novel *The Idiot* (1869), the scene at Nastasya Filippovna's name-day party erupts into a carnival-like atmosphere very soon. In *Crime and Punishment* (1866), we can see elements of a Menippean kind in Raskolnikov's first visit to Sonya, where the reading of Gospels in a slum setting sets the tone. In *The Possessed* (1872), Stavrogin's confession along with his dialogue with Tikhon takes on carnivalesque features. It is significant that crucial scenes in these novels take place in settings which involve a threshold, like a room opening to a street or street squares. In *Rabelais and His World* (1965), his book on the culture of carnival, Bakhtin explains how these are emblematic of the setting of the street which was where carnivals were staged.

DOUBLE-VOICED DISCOURSE

In the chapter, 'Discourse in Dostoevsky', Bakhtin discusses the features of double-voiced discourse in great detail. Discourse here means 'language in its concrete living totality' (*Problems of* 181). Speech differentiations of characters do not suggest dialogism. The mere presence of language styles, language diversity and social dialects do not automatically imply dialogic relations. Bakhtin writes, 'What matters is the *dialogic angle* at which these styles and dialects are juxtaposed or counterposed in the work' (182). Utterances which internalise subject positions are suggestive of dialogic relations. Every utterance carries a voice and has an author. When two voices collide within an utterance, we have a dialogic situation. When we observe our own utterance or a part of it from outside, and subject it to evaluation, we create a dialogic situation. Double-voiced discourse is discourse oriented towards the discourse of others. Stylisation, parody and *Skaz* are examples of double-voiced discourse.

Russian formalists have discussed *Skaz* in detail. In this kind of narration, the emphasis is on speech. The narrator, who was different from the author, spoke in colloquial speech. The author would use only the prevalent literary style. *Skaz* narration was common in Russian folktales, and it was known for its speech-like quality in the act of telling. Bakhtin feels that the most important feature of *Skaz* is 'its orientation towards the speech of another' (191), which was not recognised by Russian formalists. Orality was, in fact, a secondary feature, and was not central to the 'encounter between two consciousnesses'. In stylisation and parody, we find a similar 'orientation towards another's discourse, towards someone else's speech' (185). In the scientific study of language, as evidenced by disciplines like lexicography, and stylistics, these aspects of language use have not received the attention they deserve.

From this perspective, Bakhtin tries to provide an exhaustive classification of discourses of various types. First is the **direct, unmediated discourse** which refers to an external object. It is used for naming, informing or expressing and representing the intention of the speaker. This type of discourse communicates the semantic authority of the speaker.

Secondly, we have the **objectified discourse of a represented person**. The direct speech of characters is a good example of this type of discourse. This type of discourse may be dominated by social or individual features, thus displaying characteristics typical of a society or individuals.

Then comes the discourse which has an orientation towards someone else's discourse, which Bakhtin terms **double-voiced discourse**. Here, he differentiates between three varieties of such discourses. The first of this type is **unidirectional double-voiced discourse**, in which we have stylisation, narrator's narration and a character's narration which communicates the author's intentions. In the second type, **vari-directional double-voiced discourse**, we have parodies of various kinds. At one extreme, it may exist as parody with all its nuances and at the other extreme, it may be any transmission of someone else's words with a shift in accent. In the third type, **reflected discourse of another**, there is hidden internal polemic, polemically coloured autobiography or confession, any discourse with a sideward glance at someone else's word, a rejoinder of a dialogue, or hidden dialogue. In this third type, Bakhtin envisages different types of interrelationships with another's discourse. There can be various degrees of influence that one discourse has on the other.

Bakhtin revises the above classification in a later essay, 'Discourse in the Novel' (1934–35), to make it more elaborate as part of a 'Prosaics' he proposes for the novel as a form. Here, he uses the term 'internal dialogism' to distinguish it from the ordinary dialogues which happen as part of routine life. The process of dialogism involves an outward movement towards the external environment where it collides with other meanings and accents:

> The word directed towards its object enters this dialogically agitated and tension-filled environment of other words and evaluations and accents, weaves itself into their complex inter-relations, merges with some, recoils from or intersects with others; and all of this fundamentally form the word, may leave deposits in all its semantic layers, complexify what it expresses and influence its entire stylistic profile. ('Discourse in the Novel' 276)

These dimensions of the word are not captured by stylistics as a discipline. Bakhtin is highly critical of its inability to deal with double-voiced discourse in general, and its various aspects of dual directionality in particular. Stylistics tends to focus on 'direct referentially oriented discourse' (*Problems of* 200) alone. This essentially means that stylistics recognises only language used 'in a single self-enclosed context' (200). The changes that take place in the use of words as they move between utterances, or when an utterance changes its orientation are beyond the grasp of this discipline. Bakhtin writes, 'The life and functions of a word in the *style* of a concrete utterance are perceived against the background of its life and functions in *language*' (200). By doing so, the inherent dialogic potential of the word, its proclivity to remain multiple in orientations is silenced. Bakhtin feels that 'prose, and especially the novel, is completely beyond the reach of such a stylistics' (201). Words are inhabited by others' voices and this dimension of verbal utterance in literature cannot be interpreted in terms of stylistics.

The chapter on 'Discourse in Dostoevsky' ends with Bakhtin's illustrations of the use and function of the extraordinary diversity of types and varieties of discourse. Dostoevsky's fictional works such as *The Double* (1864) and *Notes from Underground* (1864) are analysed in detail here. The story *The Double* is full of questions Golyadkin asks himself. The second voice, that of the double, becomes available to him to engage with, and enables him to enter into a conversation with himself. There are endless shifts in tone and words between the hero and his double, the double taking on the accent of the real hero and sounding like him. Bakhtin comments, Dostoevsky 'forces his heroes to recognize themselves, their idea, their own words, their orientation, their gesture in another person, in whom all these phenomena change their integrated and ultimate meaning and take on a different sound, the sound of parody or ridicule' (217).

Bakhtin concludes that the entire story is constructed as an interior dialogue between three voices which takes place within a single dismantled consciousness. The same word or idea is echoed through three separate voices, and it takes on new features in each voice. Each voice is interrupted by the other and the meaning of the story can be understood only with reference to those moments of interruption.

The limitations of Bakhtin's critical study of Dostoevsky are inseparable from its strengths. Bakhtin was not a 'systematic' thinker who built an elaborate system flawlessly. However, he offers flashes of insights which can be traced to his spontaneous and inquiring way of literary investigation. His long-winded sentences often lack clarity, though this discourse can be traced to a certain Russian tradition of literary criticism. Bakhtin does not take up each novel for detailed analysis to bring out its salient features. He is led by a large overriding idea that he follows to its fullest limits, in the process of which diverse issues are examined. It is imperative to remember that in Western or Eastern poetics, the novel as a literary form was hardly subjected to any detailed analysis before Bakhtin. Western poetics focused mostly on tragic drama and dramatic forms in all their various incarnations. Indian poetics was exclusively concerned with poetry and poetic forms. Against such a background, Bakhtin's success in creating a poetics of the novel appears a formidable achievement.

It was Bakhtin's early philosophical preoccupations with neo-Kantian ideas that helped him recognise some of the basic traits of the novel. The question of 'answerability' as a primary condition of human existence enabled him to perceive the ethical dimension of dialogic forms in human interactions. The ability of the novelistic form to accommodate heteroglossia to a much greater extent, more than any other literary form, was evident to Bakhtin very early in his critical career. The anti-canonical nature of the novelistic form makes its literariness problematic. The transgressive attributes of the novel were, for the first time, traced to earlier cultural forms of Western society, such as dialogue and the carnival, by Bakhtin.

Bakhtin revised and expanded the first edition of his work on Dostoevsky while bringing out a new edition in 1963. The focus was considerably widened as Bakhtin had rethought many of his earlier ideas from different perspectives. The fourth chapter, 'Characteristics of Genre and Plot Construction in Dostoevsky's Works' was rewritten substantially, as questions of Socratic dialogues and Menippean satires were taken up for detailed examination. He had mentioned Dostoevsky's connection with European Romanticism, the differences in the way the idea of dialogue was perceived by Dostoevsky and Plato, and the relevance of the Biblical dialogue for Dostoevsky, in his first book. An important insight he excluded from the 1963 edition pertains to Dostoevsky's utopian impulse. Bakhtin comments, 'Dostoevsky's heroes are indeed motivated by the Utopian dream of creating some sort of human community that lies beyond existing social forms' (280).

He goes on to explain how Myshkin, Alyosha and other characters aspire towards establishing such Utopian communities. This desire points to 'the social disorientation of the classless intelligentsia' (281) whose members now find it necessary to re-orient themselves towards the community. Equally significant is Bakhtin's observation that 'capitalism created the conditions for a special type of inescapably solitary consciousness' (288). Dostoevsky was concerned with the falsity of this consciousness. This explains the question of violence that Dostoevsky examines in all his novels through multiple perspectives. Bakhtin comments,

> The materialization of man under conditions of class society, carried to its extreme under capitalism. This materialization is accomplished (realized) by external forces acting on the personality from without and from within; this is violence in all possible forms of its realization (economic, political, ideological) and these forces can be combated only from the outside and with equally externalized forces. (298)

Such explicit political statements are never found in Bakhtin's later works. It is possible that he could no longer justify such a blatant statement of political ideology in the discussion of Dostoevsky's novels which signified complex philosophical issues. That Bakhtin retained much of his earlier material and expanded its central argument, suggests that there is a core set of beliefs and issues behind his quest as a cultural critic.

In the chapters that follow, there will be occasions to return to Bakhtin's close readings of Dostoevsky's novels to bring out the nature and function of dialogic imagination in their narratives. Bakhtin's treatment of the concept of the carnival and its multiple manifestations in literature and art will be analysed in the next chapter.

REFERENCES

Bakhtin, Mikhail, M. *Problems of Dostoevsky's Poetics.* Edited and translated by Caryl Emerson. Introduction by Wayne C. Booth. Minneapolis: U of Minnesota P, 1984. Print.

---. 'Discourse in the Novel'. *The Dialogic Imagination: Four Essays*. Ed. Michael Holquist. Trans. Caryl Emerson and Michael Holquist. Austin: U of Texas P, 2008. Print.

Dostoevsky, Fyodor. *The Brothers Karamazov.* Trans. Constance Garnett. New York: Lowell Press, 2009. Print.

Chapter Five

Carnival and Its Ethos

IMPLICATIONS FOR LITERATURE AND CULTURE

Mikhail Bakhtin's study of the carnival culture in medieval Europe has to be seen in the context of the 1930s in Russia. Michael Holquist rightly observes, 'At one level, *Rabelais and His World* is a parable and a guidebook for its times, inexplicable without reference to the close connection between the circumstances of its own production and Soviet intellectual and political history' (*Rabelais and His World* xiv–xv). In Russia, the study of carnival culture had several predecessors. Bakhtin was part of a group of scholars that included Dmitry Zelenin, Nikolai Trubetzkoy, Roman Jakobson, Petr Bogatyrev and Vladimir Propp who closely studied the lower strata of culture as opposed to the uniform 'high culture'. Carnival is characterised by heteroglossia and its multiplicity of styles. The domain of laughter provides a space for dissent and critical rejoinder when official prohibition of certain kinds of laughter, irony and satire is imposed upon writers.

It may be noted here that carnival is central to the conceptual world of Bakhtin, as it carries forward his ideas of unfinalisability and embodiment. His essay on chronotope also refers to the carnival forms of literature. The idea of *becoming* runs through much of his discussion on the novel, the process by which the human subject resists the idea of closure. In his study of Dostoevsky, he elaborated on dialogism and polyphony with reference to language. Bakhtin was a thinker who made a difference to the way in which we conceive language. However, in his study of carnival, the material body becomes the stage for exploring a set of ideas that are related to politics, life and literature. He idealises participative life and establishes the underlying relations between artistic imagination, the everyday world and speech genres. Unlike heteroglossia, polyphony and dialogism, chronotope and carnival are ideas that have very little to do with language, to begin with. In the former, the temporal dimension is emphasised while in the latter, the physical and the material are given priority. Both chronotope and carnival are ideas that mark the period during which Bakhtin progressively refined his ideas on the origin and development of the novel. In Bakhtin's ideological world, carnival stands apart as a concept which has implications beyond literature and the arts. It has found resonance in the study of popular culture, cinema and theatre, and has initiated discussions on biopolitics in fields like feminism.

DISSENT AND TRANSGRESSION

It is important to remember that Bakhtin's book on carnival was submitted as a doctoral thesis to Gorky Institute of World Literature in Moscow, in 1940. The outbreak of the war prevented the open defense for several years. He was finally called upon to defend his thesis in 1947, before the State Commission on Degrees. He was denied a doctoral degree, though many on the committee defended him. He was awarded a degree below the doctoral level, denying him a chance to pursue an academic career. The work was finally published in Russia in 1965 under the title *François Rabelais and the Folk Culture of the Middle Ages and Renaissance.*

The Stalinist years in Russia had seen the progressive decline of intellectual dissent and collectivisation of thought and ideas. Bakhtin was convinced that the give and take between the medieval church and state on the one hand and the carnival on the other was a power struggle. He was quick to see a parallel in the 1930s in Russia. Bakhtin's book on carnival was a critical interpretation of the world he lived in. After the Russian Revolution, the nation state had arrogated to itself the power to adjudicate what is right and wrong, moral and immoral, resulting in the suppression of multiple points of view that were inherent in society. A powerful centre such as the Soviet nation state imposed a status quo, curbing the desire for change from below.

In 1934 the Communist Party had organised a series of discussions on the nature of the novel. The social realist novel was granted legitimacy in the arguments of the proceedings. Bakhtin's emphasis on 'grotesque realism' can be viewed as a refutation of the hegemonic views on 'socialist realism' expressed by the official body of the Communist Party. He inverts the categories and refutes the tenor of the arguments put forward officially. By critically examining the relations between body, language and political practice, the idea of carnival laughter explores the possibility of recovering a popular domain of dissent. In the process, Bakhtin is able to trace the origin of the European novel to the popular tradition of folklore and the collective life of the community.

RABELAIS AND HIS WORLD: A PATH-BREAKING WORK

Anatoly Lunacharsky (1875–1933), who occupied important positions in the Bolshevik government, had set up a government commission to study satiric genres (xviii). His address on satire at the Academy of Sciences in 1933 outlined its historical importance and its connections with carnival. When Bakhtin came across its published version in 1935, it inspired him to pursue the subject further. His approach to the culture of carnival differed from that of Lunacharsky, who viewed it as a safety valve for common people who were oppressed by the autocratic system. The point to be noted here is that the study of folklore and carnival culture had gone through a revival in the early 1930s in Russia.

Bakhtin's path-breaking book *Rabelais and His World* (1984) was an attempt to rewrite the cultural history of Europe from a popular perspective. He also wanted to save folklore studies from reductive and insular approaches. From his own experience, Bakhtin had come to realise that intense intellectual struggles were required to preserve freedom. What he explored was carnival laughter and its essential relation to freedom. François Rabelais (1494–1553) lived during the conjunction of the medieval age and the Renaissance period, when the history of carnival culture was still fresh in the minds of the people of Europe. It marked a moment when the popular chthonian (relating to or inhabiting the underworld) impulse to carnival could be articulated in literature. Before the emergence of the feudal system of class divisions and the Roman Catholic Church's hegemonic control over European society, the serious and the comic co-existed in the everyday life of the people. As the state's role became absolute in all matters pertaining to the life of the people, comic forms disappeared from public platforms. Once they became part of the non-official world, they came to be invested with the everyday experiences and aspirations of the common people which transformed them into an expression of folk consciousness and folk culture.

Rabelais was a renowned writer and scholar of the French Renaissance. He was a trained physician, lived the life of a monk and had attained mastery over many languages including Greek and Latin. In a series of five novels, he recounted the lives and adventures of two giants, Gargantua and his son Pantagruel, in a satirical idiom that fascinated the reader with wordplay, wisdom, satire and extensive erudition. His breadth of vision as a humanist and thinker, combined with his subtle critique of medieval institutions made his work a French classic. *Gargantua and Pantagruel* (1532–64) made extensive use of popular legends, romances and classical material from Latin, Greek and Italian. Rabelais's mock-heroic style directed against the obscurantism and hermeticism of his days, along with his remarkable felicity as a storyteller, made each of his five novels greatly popular. His flamboyant style and fearless critique of piety and orthodoxy resonated throughout Europe.

Bakhtin identifies certain distinct forms of folk culture: ritual spectacles of the marketplace consisting of carnival pageants and similar displays, comic verbal compositions like parodies, the various genres of billingsgate registers like abuses, oaths and curses, and carnival festivities including the feast. It should be kept in mind that all these different elements of carnival culture had flourished for almost a millennium before the Renaissance. By the time authors like Rabelais and Shakespeare came, they had disappeared from the common life of society. What used to be a life-giving celebration of human spirit had now been reduced to a weekend holiday kind of distraction. The spirit of carnival stayed on, despite its subjugation by official culture, in the everyday use of language and literary expressions. With the Enlightenment enforcing a regime of reason in every sphere of life from the end of the seventeenth century, the attraction for the irrational and the marginal proved irresistible. Now literature, entire cultures, came to be carnivalised. It became a source of rejuvenating literary discourse in general and novelistic genres in particular.

The Marketplace and Its Spectacles

The comic rituals of the marketplace defy the sanctity and high seriousness of ecclesiastic dogmatism. The distinction between the spectator and the actor disappears in the performative culture of the carnival. The festive culture of the carnival is inspired by an idealistic view of human existence. The feast as a temporal event is linked to moments of crisis in the cycle of nature, in the life of society and in the life of the community. The event of the feast marks an entry into the utopian realm of community, freedom, equality and abundance, and is inspired by an idealist vision of the world. Bakhtin comments, 'Moments of death and revival, of change and renewal always led to a festive perception of the world' (*Rabelais and His World* 8–9). The feast enabled people oppressed by the regime of power structures to move out of the formal links with time. The carnivalised nature of the feast challenged the unchanging, stable order of authoritarian power. Carnival was an occasion for suspension of rank, privileges, norms and prohibitions.

People in the medieval era were witness to a series of pageants and processions, feasts, satirical farces, and open-air amusements throughout the year. These were full of irreverence and transgressions of various kinds. Agricultural feasts that accompanied the harvesting of grapes were full of gaiety and abandon. Giants, dwarfs, trained animals and monsters added to the spirit of joviality on such occasions. Clowns and fools mimicked serious civic and social ceremonies like the transfer of feudal rights and the initiation of knights. It should be borne in mind that the dominant atmosphere of the medieval times was one of feudal, ecclesiastical, official seriousness. The carnivalesque atmosphere which looked at this hierarchical power structure from the outside provided a lifeline of hope and renewal to the oppressed minds of these times. People kept alive their creativity through this popular domain of transgressive activities.

During the Middle Ages, various forms of carnivalesque expressions were enacted at the marketplace. The practice of ritual spectacle lasted as long as three months in certain cities in medieval Europe. These carnivalistic celebrations were informal, unofficial, profane in spirit and loaded with political symbolism. The carnival spirit manifested itself through the dynamic playfulness of the mutable, ever-changing, undefined forms. It constructed a parallel world where the solidity of the normative was turned upside down. This is what the novels of Rabelais echo. Carnival laughter is inclusive, it does not leave anyone out. Carnival imagery in its various forms informs the works of Desiderius Erasmus (1466–1536), William Shakespeare (1564–1616), Lope de Vega (1562–1635), Luis Vélez de Guevara (1579–1644), Francisco Gómez de Quevedo (1580–1645), Johann Fischart (1545–91) and Hans Sachs (1494–1576). Bakhtin underlines the ambivalent nature of carnival laughter: 'It asserts and denies, it buries and revives' (11). Carnival laughter is critical in its orientation as it deflates and destabilises. It calls into question the official truth, 'a truth already established, the predominant truth that was put forward as eternal and indisputable' (9). Carnival provides release from the stringent 'official' life of the streets, affording a second life to the people at large, making it possible for them to reinvent their identities. Repressive regimes are suspicious of popular imagination and do everything possible to restrain their spirit. Carnival laughter has a subversive function in extending the possibilities of self-expression, dissent and critical thinking. Society can recover its mobility only if it is able to move out of its moribund state of withdrawal and isolation.

Types of Parodies

Comic verbal compositions were produced in Latin as well as in the vernacular. During carnival festivities, which sometimes lasted for nearly three months, the carnival spirit permeated the entire population. Even men of rank, theologians, monks, clerics and schoolmen participated in the production of parodies and other forms of comic compositions that used a variety of genres and styles. No ecclesiastical cult or teaching was left untouched in this subversive form of comic rendering: learned treatises, liturgies ('The Liturgy of Drunkards', 'The Liturgy of Gamblers', and so on), litanies, hymns, psalms, and even epitaphs and canonical decrees were subjected to parodies. One also comes across parodies of debates, dialogues, chronicles, and so forth. Erasmus's *In Praise of Folly* (1511) can be understood in its true spirit only if one understands the Latin tradition of carnival laughter. In the vernacular tradition, one finds the parodies of prayers, sermons, carols and legends of saints.

In an authoritarian regime, language is strictly policed by the requirements of decorum. Whereas verbal etiquette and discipline collapse in the language of the marketplace. Abusive language, profanities and oaths, which are varieties of language one encounters in the billingsgate, had their functions in magic and incantation. The official feasts always reinforced the existing power structure and demanded obedience and submission. The carnival time was one of suspension of all that was official and hierarchical. Parody was the medium through which the comic spirit penetrated the highest form of religious and feudal thought. For instance, *Coena Cypriani* (Cyprian's Supper) offered a carnivalesque parody of the entire Scriptures. Virgilius Grammaticus (Virgil the Grammarian of the seventh century) authored two grammatical texts, *Epitome* and *Epistolae*, which deviated from the style of normative grammar. Bakhtin describes his works as 'semiparodical learned treatise on Latin grammar which is at the same time a parody of the scholarly wisdom and of the scientific methods of the early Middle Ages' (14). He included anecdotes, folklore and many varieties of Latin, rendering questions of grammatical authority suspect. Such parodies could be enjoyed only if one had a good grounding in medieval traditions of scholarship. They were enjoyed by courtiers, the clergy and also scholars from the university. It is important to note that all this was tolerated by the church. It was sanctified by the tradition of 'Paschal laughter' or 'Christmas laughter'. With its penetration of high society, the lower forms of carnival laughter breached the class divide, opening up the rigid boundaries established by prevailing rules and regulations.

Behind carnival laughter is the vision that nothing in life is 'stable, unchanging, perennial, eternal and undisputable' (*Problems of* 166). It is a plea for an open and free world. Implicit in its ideology is a warning to the official powers that there are other worldviews and forces that exist outside. It has often been argued that carnivals only help to reinforce the official political culture, as they provide only temporary release in the course of the political life of a society. This line of argument can be put forward regarding any radical ideology. Carnival was a reminder that the world is not monolithic, and that beyond the visible authorities of power there are social and political forces that shape the course of history. The folk in the carnival also subject themselves to criticism and ridicule. They oppose everything that is finalised; remain in a state of flux, in a state of becoming, resisting closure.

It was during the Renaissance that vernacular literatures came into their own. The spirit of the carnival spilled over into these literatures, creating a popular foundation for their acceptance. We find parodies of prayers, sermons, Christmas carols and legends of saints in the language of the vernacular. Since the new European languages attained their maturity in this atmosphere of critical laughter, they could transmit carnival laughter to their main literary forms. The high tradition of the European languages had no problem with carnivalised forms of literary genres, mainly because they never had a high tradition of piety and orthodoxy to begin with. They assimilated the spirit of questioning and criticism which enabled them to develop worldviews grounded in the everyday world.

Language of the Marketplace

Bakhtin emphasises the centrality of the market square as an important chronotope in the history of the novel. Many important scenes in Dostoevsky's novels take place in the street or market square. It was in the medieval carnivalised genres that the marketplace and the street became an important setting for staging folk humour.

The familiar speech of the marketplace consisted of abusive words, words with double meanings, offensive expressions and obscenities. Bakhtin feels these were derived from a longer tradition of folk humour where such language played a significant role in the rituals of black magic and performance traditions of incantations. Laughter signifies the death of the old world and the birth of a new world. The material images of the lower part of the body signify the process of regeneration. Bakhtin comments, 'they debase, destroy, regenerate, and renew simultaneously. . . . Death and death throes, labor, and childbirth are intimately interwoven' (*Rabelais and His World* 151). There are cults which mock and insult the deity as part of their rituals. Thus, the speech used in the marketplace could be traced back to primitive human societies. The ambivalence of their usage was partly derived from their multiple uses in different locations. In the carnivalised spectacle this kind of language became secularised. Profanities and oaths were also assimilated into the language of the marketplace as the street square attained the dimensions of a theatre. They all enriched the carnival atmosphere.

One of the specific features of street life was the street cries. This was how vendors advertised their wares, which included every type of food and wine. Paris street life comes alive in the works of Rabelais when he documents the street cries. This culture was suffused with loud spoken words of various tones. In Rabelais, the commercial advertising of the apothecary, actor, quack, astrologer and barker all contribute to the pandemonium of the street. Bakhtin comments, 'The cries of Paris represented in themselves a noisy kitchen and a loud, abundantly served banquet; every dish had its own rhyme and melody' (218). The Protestants used the metaphor of the kitchen to mock and satirise the Catholic Church in the well-known 'Christian Satires on the Papal Kitchen' (*Satyres chrestiennes de la cuisine papale*, 1560). Prayers and rituals become foods of various kinds. Grotesque realism of this kind debases and debunks. In the modern period, Émile Zola and Victor Hugo have deployed some of these images in their writings. While describing his voyage down the Rhine, Hugo mentions an inn in these words: 'If I were Homer or Rabelais, I would say that this kitchen is a world and this chimney its sun' (qtd. in *Rabelais and His World* 184).

In Rabelais, images of the kitchen and the hearth attain universal meanings.

Studies of folk literature, particularly in India, have failed to use the insights provided by Bakhtin regarding carnivalised spectacles. Rituals and spectacles have often been studied without reference to the contexts of carnival they belong to. While studying the comic and travestying genres it is important to keep in mind their medieval origin. They were often viewed solely in modern contexts, and this prevented critics from exploring their full potential. Rabelais has often been accused of exaggerating the physical and the scatological. Victor Hugo described him as the greatest poet of the 'flesh' and 'belly' (125–26). We forget that similar traits can be observed in the works of Renaissance authors such as Giovanni Boccaccio, Shakespeare and Cervantes. The explanation offered by modern critics was that they were reacting to medieval piety from a Renaissance standpoint. But Bakhtin strongly argues that these traits are part of a complete vision of life: 'They are the heritage of that peculiar type of imagery and, more broadly speaking, of that peculiar aesthetic concept which is characteristic of this folk culture and which differs sharply from the aesthetic concept of the following ages. We shall call it conditionally the concept of grotesque realism' (*Rabelais and His World* 205).

The bulk of Bakhtin's work on Rabelais deals with the concept of grotesque realism in its philosophical and literary aspects.

Grotesque Realism

While the features of culture outlined above had been studied in Europe at various stages, they were not seen as part of carnival culture and its historical evolution. Rabelais's work repeatedly returns to the human body in all its physical aspects, to defecation and sexuality in particular. The images of the material body are a legacy of the culture of folk humour. The term 'grotesque realism' is an important addition to the critical vocabulary derived from Bakhtin. It is primarily concerned with the aesthetic features of the representation of the material body. The body is seen here in continuation with the earth, the world and society. It is not individuated but seen as part of a larger whole. Bakhtin writes,

'This is why all that is bodily becomes grandiose, exaggerated, immeasurable' (19). It points to the world of fertility, growth and abundance. Carnival culture cannot be quantified in terms of the productivity of the 'economic man' as it embodies the collective body of all the people. The defining feature of grotesque realism is 'degradation, that is, the lowering of all that is high, spiritual, ideal, abstract' (19). This can be seen in the role of the gestures of the clown who transferred the gestures of high ceremony or ritual to the material sphere, debasing it in the process. Don Quixote's actions become intelligible in the light of the carnival of degradation. The primary function of parody is to degrade and bring down to earth all that is held in high esteem, like high art and literature.

Grotesque realism emphasises the realm of the reproductive lower stratum, which is associated with conception and new birth. While parody, in general, has a negative character, medieval parody was regenerative. Sancho plays the role of a critical parodist to the role of the high-flown idealist that Don Quixote plays. In *Don Quixote* (1605), appearances are deceptive. This transformative logic derives from the culture of the carnival. Renaissance realism did not represent the material body in individualist terms: 'Bodies could not be considered for themselves; they represented a material bodily whole and therefore transgressed the limits of their isolation' (23). The carnival spirit accounts for the inclusive and the collective. The bourgeois concept of the 'completed atomized being' is held in conflict with the 'ever-growing, inexhaustible, ever-laughing principle which uncrowns and renews' (24).

The history of social realism has to be understood in relation to the tradition of grotesque realism that preceded it in the medieval period and even earlier. The vitality of the carnivalised language, embodied by oaths and abuses, has been lost in modern times. The tradition of the grotesque dates back to the ancient times. The grotesque runs parallel to the classic, Bakhtin observes (30). They did not exist in complete isolation. Even during the Renaissance when the classical had attained canonical status, the grotesque interacted with the classical. In Rabelais, one could find classical elements. With the Renaissance, the perception of the body had changed. The unfinished nature of the body (characteristic of grotesque realism) with its protuberances, convexities and apertures was found incompatible with its 'aesthetics of the beautiful' now. Bakhtin observes, 'The accent was placed on the completed, self-sufficient individuality of the given body' (29). The hideous and formless body of grotesque realism was forgotten in the classical age. The grotesque canon defies the concept of order and perfection, and by its very nature is non-canonical. During the classical period, the grotesque was banished from the official domain to lower art forms. The summit of grotesque realism was achieved in the literature of the Renaissance.

In order to understand the significance of the lower strata of the body in the descriptions of Rabelais, one has to note its function in the larger narrative. Bakhtin notes that in Rabelais, all the warm medicinal springs of France and Italy were generated by the hot urine of the sick Pantagruel. Orion (the word in Greek has a root which means 'to urinate') is given birth through the urine of Jupiter, Neptune and Mercury. The chamber pot becomes the source of much wordplay through its euphemisms. The images of urine and feces are linked to the underworld which has regenerative potential. All that is sublime is degraded here, but it also simultaneously regenerates and renews. In modern times, what we fail to recognise is that the scatological and the physical are part of a larger symbolic system rooted in a complete vision of life. These were never part of the mainstream high literary traditions of Europe. As Bakhtin observes, 'In all world literature there is probably no other work reflecting so fully and deeply all aspects of the life of the marketplace as does Rabelais' novel' (213).

THE LEGACY OF RABELAIS

With the rise and domination of the classical canon in the seventeenth and eighteenth centuries, grotesque realism came to be excluded from great literature. The state, which became the arbitrator of culture, turned festive life into official parades. Festivities were now confined to the family's private life. The grotesque lost its living relationship with folk culture and became a literary genre. The grotesque images derived from carnival traditions became formalised, which enabled them to survive in many forms and contexts. Bakhtin observes that 'the contents of the carnival-grotesque element, its artistic, heuristic, and unifying forces were preserved in all essential manifestations during the seventeenth and eighteenth centuries' (34) in the works of Molière, Voltaire, Diderot and Swift, apart from the comic novels and travesties of the seventeenth century.

In the second half of the eighteenth century, scholars such as Justus Möser and Carl Friedrich Flögel made attempts to study carnival culture. During the Romantic period, the grotesque was revived and it became the 'expression of subjective, individualistic world outlook very different from the carnival folk concept of previous ages, although still containing some carnival elements' (36). Bakhtin cites Laurence Sterne's *Tristram Shandy* (1759) as a 'peculiar transposition of Rabelais' and Cervantes' world concept into the subjective language of the new age' (37). The Gothic or the Black novel was another example of the new form of grotesque literature. Bakhtin feels that the Romantic grotesque was a reaction against the 'cold rationalism' and the 'official, formalistic, and logical authoritarianism' of the classical period. The didactic and utilitarian aspects of the Enlightenment were overturned in this worldview. This age also rediscovered the significance of Cervantes and Shakespeare from a new perspective. While the medieval and Renaissance grotesque had its roots in carnival culture, the Romantic grotesque was individualistic and subjective. While the grotesque principle of laughter was transgressive and subversive, in the Romantic period the comic lost its hilarity, and 'was reduced to cold humor, irony, sarcasm' (38). The regenerative force of laughter was thus lost. This also makes the world of the Romantic grotesque 'a terrifying world, alien to man' (38). The ordinary world loses its significance, as it is reduced to an alien world. Images of worldly life turned into vulgarities. The links with folk culture enabled the grotesque of the medieval period to conquer the negative forces of fear but in the Romantic period, the grotesque seemed to inspire terror in the reader.

The theme of madness recurs in the literature of the grotesque. While in the medieval carnival forms, madness was 'gay parody of official reason, of the narrow seriousness of official "truth"' (39), this festive element is lost in the Romantic grotesque where it becomes tragic, a sign of individual isolation. Our everyday world becomes an alien world in this tradition. The capacity of laughter to defeat terror was a defining feature of folk-carnival, but this conception has been progressively lost in the subsequent centuries. Bakhtin observes that in the second half of the nineteenth century, interest in the grotesque waned. However, in the twentieth century, with the emergence of modernism, there was a renewed interest in the grotesque. Two strands are visible in the development of the grotesque during this phase. While certain aspects of the Romantic grotesque found deeper expression in modernist literature—in existentialist writing in particular—the realist grotesque makes its presence felt in the writings of Thomas Mann, Pablo Neruda and Bertolt Brecht. Of these writers, Brecht comes closest to the folk tradition of the earlier carnival culture. Bakhtin discusses at length, a study of grotesque by Wolfgang Kayser titled *The Grotesque in Painting and Poetry* (1961). For Kayser, the grotesque is 'something hostile, alien and inhuman' (47). He stresses the fact that the world of the grotesque is an alienated world. It is the world of the id. Bakhtin finds that the views of Kayser take into account only Romantic and modernist literatures. The larger history of folk humour which is basic to a carnivalised sense of the world, hardly figures in his critical account.

Bakhtin's immediate interest in *Rabelais and His World* is Rabelais's work, medieval folk humour and its various manifestations. He comments that 'Rabelais' work is an encyclopedia of folk culture' (58). To understand Rabelais's exceptional charm, Bakhtin feels it is necessary to 'understand his peculiar language, that is, the language of the culture of the folk humor' (58).

THE HISTORY OF LAUGHTER

In his work, Bakhtin evaluates Rabelais's contribution to the history of laughter. Rabelais's works were greatly appreciated by his contemporaries. *Gargantua and Pantagruel* was popular with its readers, judging by the enthusiastic comments from his contemporaries. The work also had an impact on serious writers of the times. Rabelais's deeper relations with folk culture could be understood by his contemporaries. They shared the same world and hence they could grasp 'the wholeness and order of the Rabelaisian aesthetic and ideological world' (61–62). However, as folk culture receded from memory, readers of the sixteenth and seventeenth centuries began to view his works as rooted in 'some strange individual idiosyncracy' (62). What was self-evident to his contemporaries became a manifestation of a secret code to the writers of later ages. When Rabelaisian works are viewed as satires, they are misread. Bakhtin observes, 'When the grotesque is used to illustrate an abstract idea, its nature is inevitably distorted. The essence of the grotesque is precisely to present a contradictory and double-faced fullness of life. Negation and destruction (death of the old) are included as an essential phase, inseparable from affirmation, from the birth of something new and better' (62).

Abstract ideas shifted the centre of gravity of the grotesque to a moral meaning. This process deepened in subsequent centuries. By the end of the sixteenth century, Rabelais was completely sidelined from the list of serious literature and by the seventeenth century he was seen as a 'merely amusing and gay author' (65). Montaigne terms Boccaccio's *Decameron,* Rabelais's works, and *Basia* by Jean Second 'simply amusing works' (qtd. in *Rabelais and His World* 65). However, for Montaigne, the amusing was not an inferior category. Rabelais, Cervantes and Shakespeare are writers who understood that laughter has a philosophical meaning. Laughter enables us to see life from a new perspective. The Renaissance conception of laughter was that 'certain essential aspects of the world are accessible only to laughter' (66). From the seventeenth century onwards, laughter came to be seen not as a universal, philosophical form but only as an individual phenomenon of social life. The comic was now seen as a narrow sphere pertaining to the private and social vices. It was believed that the literature of the comic belonged to the low genres as it could not convey 'the essential truth about the world' (67).

Bakhtin traces the history of laughter to the ancient Greek writer Menippus (third century BCE), whose satires became a model for the subsequent writings of Lucian, the ancient

Greek satirist, and Renaissance writers of Italy. In the satires of Menippus, the prevalent philosophical ideas of Epicureans and Stoics were subjected to criticism through irony and satire. Many of his writings took the form of dialogues which were set in the underworld. We have already discussed the role of Menippean satires in the evolution of the novel in the previous chapter.

The writings of Rabelais, Cervantes and Shakespeare are informed by the history of laughter which dates back to the pre-Christian era. During the Renaissance, the discourse of laughter was fertilised by humanist traditions of knowledge as well. The rites, rituals and feasts of the church in the medieval times were immersed in the theme of bodily regeneration and renewal. The lower bodily stratum which had the potential for transformation could not express itself in the official cult and ideology. The Middle Ages accommodated laughter both in the culture of the middle classes and the high circles of the church. This was because of the strong popular appeal of folk culture. The official culture was still at a formative stage at the time and the feudal system which was in its early stages was still relatively progressive. It is also relevant to note that folk culture had in its lineage, elements of ancient pagan celebrations. The festive laughter marks a point of transition and transformation where the past and future meet. All that is timeless, stable and established in human creations is rejected by the tradition of the grotesque. In the feasts of the fools and the ass, and on similar occasions, the hierarchy of power was reversed. Often the jester was proclaimed king or queen. Often the pontiff, the bishop or the pastor was chosen for the day to caricature their activities. All this was accompanied by a massive output of parodic literature. Parody cut across all ecclesiastical themes, cults and rituals. One comes across the 'Liturgy of the Gamblers', the 'Liturgy of the Drunkards', 'The Gambler's Gospel' and 'The Drunkard's Gospel'. Even wills and epitaphs were parodied. Bakhtin observes, 'Everything they touched was transformed into flesh and matter, and at the same time was given a lighter tone' (83).

The culture of folk communicates a deep distrust of official versions of reality and their truth claims. Along with universalism and fear, the celebration of victory over fear constituted a defining feature of the medieval carnival. In his article on Rabelais, Alexander Veselovsky argues that in the Middle Ages, 'the clown is the lawless herald of the objectively abstract truth' (qtd. in *Rabelais and His World* 93). The conventional structure of society ordained the nature of truth. This meant that all 'general human truth' which was not sanctioned by authority was excluded from official sanction. It could be tolerated if it was considered funny, as, for example, the speech of the clown. In evoking laughter, the clown also conquered fear. Laughter was opposed to dogmas and authoritarianism. In the Middle Ages, the official and the carnival lives were parallel, not merging, but co-existent. By the end of the Middle Ages, humour penetrates the domain of great literature, resulting in the creation of new genres, such as moralities, farces and *soties.* Medieval laughter informs the novels of Rabelais, constituting its inner core of critical historical consciousness (97). The forms of medieval laughter 'uncrowned and renewed the established power and official truth' (99).

A new dispensation took over the relations between politics and culture in the seventeenth century. Monarchy established a stable order which demanded a new approach to questions of culture and freedom. The rationalist philosophy of Descartes and the aesthetics of classicism reflect the fundamental traits of the new official culture. It was authoritarian and serious, despite being less dogmatic. The ambivalence of grotesque realism was not welcome anymore. In the new official culture, there was a tendency towards stability and completion of being. The defining trait of the new order was monologism, endorsement of a single meaning. The new genres that emerged in the seventeenth century distanced themselves from the influence of the grotesque. However, in the 'lower' canonical genres such as comedy, satire and fable, as well as the non-canonical genre of the novel, the grotesque continued to exert its influence. These genres had in common a shared sense of resistance to the prevailing orthodoxies. Court festivals, masquerades and ballets of the seventeenth century were spectacles with carnival traits. This shows that Rabelais's images were understood in these times. They had migrated from the marketplace to the court, and their style and meanings had undergone widespread changes.

Goethe was one writer who had extensively studied the traditional forms of spectacles. He was in charge of such performances at the court of the Weimar Republic. The popular festive imagery had a profound influence on Goethe's writings. The core vision of carnival laughter related to the material body was now transformed into erotic frivolity, with none of its utopian philosophical power. In the development of the comic novel in the seventeenth century one can see another level of development of popular festive heritage.

With the gradual penetration of Enlightenment rationality in all spheres of life in Europe, the context of Rabelais vanished from France completely. He was now 'a strange and solitary author' who had to be annotated to be understood (107). His books were rich with personal and topical allusions which were not understood by common readers. The encyclopedic range of the subjects treated in his works also demanded knowledge of several fields. The Variorum Edition (1823–26) of Rabelais's complete works in nine volumes offered the most exhaustive interpretations of Rabelais. This historical–allegorical reading of his works has not been approved by many Rabelais scholars. Such an approach only confirms the disintegration of the culture of laughter that prevailed in Europe before the Renaissance. Carnival culture continued to serve as a source of forms, themes and symbols in the eighteenth and nineteenth centuries. However, the positive associations of laughter were no more available to the audience of the modern period. During the French Revolution, Rabelais's works underwent a revival, as he was seen as a critic of monarchy. But Bakhtin feels that such an interpretation was based on false premises (120). Rabelais had a vision which was rooted in the ambivalence of laughter.

Here Bakhtin underlines the fact that the division of literary genres into high and low, where the high implies the sublime and the serious, is a development of the modern times. Tragedy, as it developed in antiquity, accommodated laughter within its structure. Euripides's *Alcestis* (438 BCE) consisted of a satirical play as the fourth drama, after the tragic trilogy. Shakespeare's tragedies accommodated laughter within their tragic structure. This is because the tragic drama as practised by these visionary writers did not admit a dogmatic vision. As Bakhtin observes, 'Laughter does not permit seriousness to atrophy and to be torn away from the one being, forever incomplete' (123). In the Age of Antiquity, no such sharp distinction was maintained by official and folk cultures. The dialogues of Socrates provide another instance of the use of laughter in the context of the serious; in this case, that of critical philosophy.

EXAMPLES FROM INDIA

The tradition of grotesque realism is indeed ancient. Bakhtin mentions the terracotta figurines discovered at Kerch, on the Crimean Peninsula, depicting 'senile pregnant hags' who were laughing (*Rabelais and His World* 25). In one of the scenes depicted in the Ajanta paintings in India, one can see a monk giving a sermon, while the members of the audience are engaged in activities like stealing fruits and playing pranks on each other, decentring the main perspective of piety and seriousness. There are several folk art forms across India such as Jatra, Tamasha, Nautanki, Bhavai, Chhau, Terukkuttu, Theyyam, Yakshagana, Rasleela and Ramlila, where carnivalised laughter is an essential component of the enactment of the main plot on the stage. In many of these performances, we come across the figure of 'Vidushaka' (the clown) who has an important role. He often carries the burden of the entire performance, linking its various segments. 'Koothu' is an art form from Kerala which uses extensive carnivalisation of mythology to comment on topical issues. 'Chakyar', the actor who narrates the story through song, storytelling and performance, uses his painted face as a mask and alludes to the topical events with irony, while enacting mythological events. He has the freedom to mock anyone in the audience, including the king. Another example of carnivalised laughter is the art form 'Thullal', wherein the dancer narrates the story through a verse narrative. Kunchan Nambiar, who is supposed to have shaped this art form with elements derived from several folk traditions, digresses from the main narrative to satirise the caste hierarchy, subjecting the nairs and namboodiris—two major castes of Kerala—to scathing invective.

Early novels in Indian languages like *Indulekha* (1889) by O. Chandu Menon, written in Malayalam, and *Chha mana atha guntha*

(Six Acres and a Third) by Fakir Mohan Senapati, written in Odia in 1896, have long sections of carnivalised portrayals. Senapati's novel extensively uses a double-voiced ironic discourse that points to the contestations of power in the emergent social order. An Indian English novel that remains a stunning achievement in the tradition of carnivalised laughter is *All About H. Hatterr* (1948) by G. V. Desani. It questions the very idea of 'Englishness' of the English language by Indianising it in its intonation, accent and vocabulary. Its use of a double-voiced discourse is directed against the ideological baggage of colonialism associated with the English language. English studies in India became 'a mask of conquest' as the language was complicit with the colonial authorities in promoting and legitimating their imperial designs on India. English became the language of modernity and material advancement with a civilising mission (Viswanathan xix). Desani demystifies English and punctures its aura as a language of power. A close reading of the novel will reveal several elements of grotesque realism which have been discussed above. Desani's use of English anticipates the polyphonic elements used by Rushdie many years later. As Rushdie explains, 'This is the babu-English, the semi-literate, half-learnt English of the bazaars, transmuted by erudition, high-brow monkeying around, and the impish magic of Desani's unique phrasing and rhythm into an entirely new kind of literary voice' (Rushdie).

The journeys of H. Hatterr (where 'H' stands for 'Hindustanwala') are reminiscent of picaresque narratives. In the novel, he meets several sages: the sages of Calcutta, Rangoon (now resident in India), Madras, Bombay, the 'right Honourable Sage of Delhi', the 'wholly Worshipful of Mogalsarai-Varanasi', 'his naked Holiness Number One, the Sage of All India himself', and three women. Each of these encounters ends in fiasco, revealing the fraudulent nature of the fake gurus parading as the great sages of modern India. The orientalist myth of India being a land of wisdom and great sages had been reinforced by colonial discourses in the nineteenth and twentieth centuries. What Desani debunks is the very myth of ancient India as the pinnacle of all wisdom. During the colonial period, Orientalists and Indologists created an aura about the classical age in India, using the Sanskrit classics. It is this myth that is parodied and degraded in the course of Desani's novel. Such an act not only deconstructs orientalist myths but also decolonises English, 'vernacularising' it.

The following extract from a section of the novel provides a sense of the carnivalisation of language that Desani uses in the novel:

> The name is H. Hatterr, and I am continuing.
>
> Biologically, I am fifty-fifty of the species.
>
> One of my parents was a European, Christian-by-faith merchant merman (seaman). From which part of the continent? Wish I could tell you. The other was an Oriental, a Malay Peninsula-resident lady, a steady, non-voyaging, non-Christian human (no mermaid). From which part of the Peninsula? Couldn't tell you either. (31)

In the high tradition of Hindu philosophy as outlined in the Upanishads, the disciple seeks out a guru for enlightenment and engages him in discussions on questions of ultimate truth. This framework is parodied by the author by combining it with picaresque conventions. The use of 'vernacularised' English in all its eccentric forms, degrades and materialises the high seriousness of abstract discourses which parades as 'spiritual'. The novel succeeds in travestying two centres of power in postcolonial India, namely the language of colonialism and the tall claims of Hindu philosophy as the ultimate source of wisdom and knowledge. It opens up a genuinely postcolonial worldview rooted in the history of people's struggle against hegemonic structures of power.

The vision of the carnival suggests that there are no eternal and ultimate truths. The semiotics of the carnival, at the level of language, theme, tone or gesture, unseat and debunk traditions and discourses held in high esteem. Rabelais, for Bakhtin, exemplifies all the aspects of the carnival spirit, in language, vision and philosophy. The parodying–travestying tradition of carnival played a pivotal role in the development of the novel in Europe and the rest of the world. One can trace elements of grotesque realism in several authors across various world languages: James Joyce, Ralph Ellison, Milan Kundera, Gabriel García Márquez and Joseph Heller are among them. Shakespeare's portrayal of Falstaff, who inverts the value system of monarchy and the feudal system, demands close examination as a stunning use of the tropes of the carnival. Many twentieth-century dramatists such as Bertolt Brecht, Samuel Beckett and Harold Pinter have successfully used elements of carnival in their theatre as well. The larger symbolism of carnival as a discursive system has to do with fertility, regeneration and renewal, and hence it runs through the entirety of human history as a subliminal force, offering an alternative value system which can create a space of resistance to absolute authority and its vicious after-effects.

The above exposition of the culture of the carnival through the ages and its embodiment in the novelistic genres prepares us for the next chapter on Bakhtin's theory of the novel. We will examine *The Dialogic Imagination: Four Essays*, to bring out the relations between the epic and the novel, the prehistory of the novelistic discourses and the idea of the chronotope and its implications for the study of literature. Bakhtin's perspectives on ethics and aesthetics will also find mention here.

REFERENCES

Bakhtin, Mikhail. *Problems of Dostoevsky's Poetics.* Edited and translated by Caryl Emerson. Introduction by Wayne C. Booth. Minneapolis: U of Minnesota P, 1984. Print.

---. *Rabelais and His World*. Trans. Hélène Iswolsky. 1968. Bloomington: Indiana UP, 1984. Print.

Clark, Katerina, and Michael Holquist. *Mikhail Bakhtin*. Cambridge, MA: The Belknap Press (Harvard UP), 1984. Print.

Desani, G. V. *All About H. Hatterr.* New Delhi: Penguin Classics, 1981. Print.

Kayser, Wolgang. *The Grotesque in Art and Literature*. McGraw-Hill, 2016. Print.

Rushdie, Salman. *Step Across this Line*. London: Random House, 2008. Kindle file.

Veselovsky, Alexander N. *Collected Articles*. Leningrad: Goslitizdat, 1939. Print.

Viswanathan, Gauri. *Masks of Conquest: Literary Study and British Rule in India*. New York: Columbia UP, 2015. Print.

Chapter Six

A Theory of the Novel

DIALOGIC IMAGINATION, HETEROGLOSSIA, CHRONOTOPE AND DISCOURSE IN THE NOVEL

Bakhtin's *The Dialogic Imagination: Four Essays* first appeared in 1975 and was translated and published in English in 1981. He had already written his critical analysis of Dostoevsky's novels before he began writing this book. In the revised edition of *Problems of Dostoevsky's Poetics*, published in 1963, he had come to view the Dostoevskian novel not as a unique event in the history of literature, but as a development that brought out the inherent possibilities of the novelistic genre to its fullest extent. Bakhtin had extensively revised and refined his views on the novel during the period between 1920 and 1960, and his mature thoughts are distilled in a series of essays he wrote in the 1950s and 60s. He is particularly concerned with the question of heteroglossia and its impact on literary genres in these essays. It must be noted that Bakhtin's ideas on the novel carry forward some of the views articulated by authors such as Georg Lukács, Friedrich Schlegel and Georg Wilhelm Friedrich Hegel. The novel as a unique genre that fulfills the possibilities inherent in dialogised discourses marks a departure in the study of the novel and provides a new critical vocabulary to discuss its form. The formal attributes of the novel had largely been ignored in twentieth-century Western criticism. New Criticism and stylistics had cultivated critical practices that examined small fragments of the text, rather than the text as a whole. Their methodology suited the study of the lyric and fragments of prose and fiction.

Novelisation is a process that had been a part of the cultural history of Europe for extended periods in the past. It is fundamentally opposed to canonisation and the politics of power relations in a hierarchical society. This had not been noted by literary historians before Bakhtin. Bakhtin outlines this process in his essay 'Epic and the Novel'. Critics such as Georg Lukács, Erich Auerbach and Lucien Goldmann who have studied the novel extensively, have failed to note the anti-canonical elements in the novel as a genre. Auerbach talks about the 'absolute' language of the Bible, but does not see it as 'monologic' in its orientation. Bakhtin finds that the novel existed in many forms in the past, but was not considered part of the hierarchy of canonised literary forms. This is because of the methodology adopted by literary critics, who solely dealt with those forms that had been completed and perfected. Literary forms such as the epic, tragedy and lyric had grown to their fullest possible extent, and had ceased to be flexible and open to the world. It is difficult to add to what Aristotle has already discussed on these forms in his *Poetics.*

The novel is the youngest literary genre, younger than print and writing. The novel resists all definitions and, unlike other genres which have greater cohesion and stability, remains more fluid and flexible. The novel belongs to the modern world and is not part of the harmonic unity of literary genres which are already part of history. In major literary periods of the past, such as the classical period of ancient Greece, the golden age of Roman literature and the neoclassical period, the novel existed as an 'unofficial' genre. Since it was outside the canon of 'high' literary genres, it was never subjected to any serious study or included in any theoretical analysis. All literary genres that are part of the high literary tradition reinforce one another. The novel was not part of this harmony of genres. Literary history tends to integrate literary works into an organic whole, but its hierarchical organisation had no place for novels.

Novelistic genres found no mention in the poetics of Aristotle, Horace or Boileau, since they insisted on the harmonious interaction of all genres. Even in the nineteenth century, those critics who had worked on issues in poetics were 'system builders' who were eclectic and descriptive. Bakhtin is critical of their 'abstract and encyclopedic comprehensiveness' (*The Dialogic Imagination* 4). They are unable to see how genres of a particular period coexist 'within the living whole of a literature in a given era' (5). Having developed along a different trajectory, the novel has little in common with other forms in terms of formal features. Its ability to assimilate the contingent and the contemporary adds to its distinctiveness. Furthermore, the novel parodies other genres within its structure, as well as exposes the conventionality of other genres. When the novel gains the upper hand in an era, other genres tend to get 'novelised'.

Novelisation is a process which Bakhtin sees in the dialogisation of other genres. In this process, other genres get dialogised, and permeated with laughter, irony, humour and elements of self-parody. Through the process of novelisation, genres which were finalised and canonised come into living contact with 'unfinished, still-evolving contemporary reality' (7). In the plays of Henrik Ibsen and in Romantic narrative poems such as Lord Byron's *Childe Harold's Pilgrimage* (1812) and *Don Juan* (1819), we have examples of such novelisation as they deviate from the generic protocols of their respective forms. As the novel is a genre still in a state of becoming, it is essentially unfinalised. This is the reason why it is interwoven with evolving contemporary reality in its contingent form. Since the novel is still in its formative stage, it can comprehend reality as a process.

The inadequacy of literary theory to understand the novel and deal with it is obvious from its descriptions of the novel. Experts on the novel tend to view it as a completed genre. They identify a single, stable characteristic of the novel and project it as the defining element of all novelistic genres. Statements like 'the novel is a prose genre' or 'the novel is a love story' do not add to our understanding of the novel as a genre. The novel can be in verse, and love is one of the many themes that may figure in the novel. Novelists such as Jean-Jacques Rousseau, Henry Fielding and Christoph Martin Wieland have provided definitions that are based on their own ideas of the novel. Hegel's theory of the novel follows the same pattern without breaking any new ground.

Bakhtin emphasises that the novel is a genre that is critical as well as self-critical. Its unique characteristics can be highlighted in comparison with the epic, which is a canonised form. Firstly, the novel is characterised by stylistic three-dimensionality. This is because it is able to embody the multilingual consciousness to the fullest extent, unlike the epic. Secondly, the novel as a form effects a radical change in its temporal coordinates. Thirdly, it is the form that has the maximum contact with the present, as is evident from its 'open-endedness'. The epic emerged in an older society when languages in Europe stayed in isolation, with very little contact with one another. Bakhtin describes the earlier closed societies as 'culturally deaf and semi-patriarchal' (12).

However, a rupture took place in European culture as it emerged into the modern times. The socially isolated communities were now open to international and interlingual contact. The world had become irreversibly polyglot: polyglossia and heteroglossia became the essential conditions of literary creation. As the world became interconnected and societies became irreversibly polyglot, languages began to see themselves in the light of other languages. Literary genres such as the tragedy, epic and lyric which were internally finalised and had ceased to grow, were also affected by the emergent interactive heteroglossia. When languages learn to share and know each other, there is a state of 'inter-illumination' between them. Polyglossia (which refers to 'multi-languagedness', or the coexistence of multiple languages in a specific society or area) now pierces languages from within and without. A language attains self-consciousness under the gaze of another language, and in the modern period the novel was born in such a context of self-consciousness. Languages are transformed from the outside as their inbuilt 'monoglossia' is breached by the heteroglossia of the modern times. The internal stratification of the novel is now available for criticism as it is subjected to analysis.

EPIC AND THE NOVEL

Territorial dialects, social and professional registers, jargons, literary languages, generational differences in language, generic languages with several types of literary languages, all constitute a rich domain of plurality in a language. The novel is the only literary form which has been able to embody this heteroglossia in its very structure. The polyglot and heteroglot conditions of language make the novel possible. The epic as a form deals with the national past which is already closed and final. This absolute past does not allow any revisions or reimaginings. The national tradition serves as the source of the epic. Its absolute epic distance from contemporary reality is characteristic of its worldview. The epic speaks of a world of fathers and founders of families. The represented world of the epic belongs to an evaluative plane which is not accessible to the contemporary reader or listener. Separated by the epic distance, its heroic time is sealed off from the present.

In his essay 'From the Prehistory of Novelistic Discourse', Bakhtin deals with the long history of 'parodic-travestying literature' predating the European novel. This kind of literature was never part of literary history as it was not part of the 'high' literary tradition. Moreover, this 'low' literature problematised the 'high' tradition and cultivated a critical attitude towards its worldviews. The satyr plays, which were performed as part of the tragic trilogy or the medieval parodies of Scriptures, are examples of such 'parodic-travestying literature'. Bakhtin refers to them as 'homeless', as they could not be pinned down to a specific social location and floated across cultural boundaries (59).

No critic before Bakhtin had been able to recognise the stylistic originality of the novel in dealing with polyglossia and heteroglossia. As mentioned above, the epic as a form defies personal interpretation. It is impossible to rethink or re-evaluate it. It is 'completed, conclusive and immutable as a fact, an idea and value' (29). While the source of the epic is memory, the novel derives from experience and knowledge. The novel is a genre 'in a state of becoming', as it is in touch with reality. The present has no essence, as it is still in the making. The novel communicates the relativity of the past while the epic represents it as absolute and final. As the novel becomes the dominant genre of the age, epistemology gains the status of a central discipline. The question of 'I, myself, my time' renders the novelistic genre open-ended. It is here that the question of ambivalent laughter assumes significance.

SERIO-COMIC GENRES

In this essay, the history of serio-comic genres once again engages Bakhtin's attention. These genres mark an important step in the evolution of the novel. Laughter is inherently inimical to the tone of the epic as it destroys the sense of hierarchical distance. Laughter demands proximity, and dispels fear and piety. Laughter and popular speech make the world free and scientifically knowable. It destroys the epic distance. Bakhtin comments that memory and tradition are not compatible with the comic; one ridicules in order to forget. The novel is concerned with the unofficial and the informal in all its multiple forms. It deals with the contemporary. It was the low forms that chose contemporary life as their subject matter. The absolute past of gods is subjected to parody in low genres. There is a long list of such serio-comic genres in the classical age: the mimes of Sophron, bucolic poems, the fable, memoir literature, pamphlets, Socratic dialogues, Roman satires, Menippean satires and Lucian's satirical dialogues. They predate the novel and portend its emergence. Friedrich Schlegel had described Socratic dialogues as the 'novels of their time' (qtd. in *The Dialogic Imagination* 22).

There is a shift from the sacred to the profane in the comical genres. What is normally elevated as the object of reverential praise, is brought down to the plane of the ordinary for analysis and criticism. Commenting on the Socratic dialogues, Bakhtin says that it arises as 'a genre of the memoir type, as transcripts based on personal memories of real conversations among contemporaries' (24). The genre revolves around the image of a speaking and conversing man. Socratic dialogues were compiled based on the transcripts of real conversations among contemporaries. Socrates wears the mask of a fool as well as that of a wise man in these dialogues. They use a variety of styles including dialects, parodied language and the well-known Socratic irony. The Socratic way of debunking prevailing myths is through familiarising them to investigate them openly and fearlessly. Menippean satires are also closely aligned with Socratic dialogues and both go back to folk roots. The wild and fantastic plots of Menippean satires critically examine the world of ideas and ideologues. Nikolai Gogol's *Dead Souls* (1842) was modelled on Dante's *Divine Comedy* (1472) but, as the form of the novel took over, it became more of a Menippean satire. What must be underlined is that the treatment of the past in the novel does not render it the 'absolute past'. The temporal model followed by the novel undergoes a major change. In the novel, there is neither a first word nor a last word.

Xenophon's *Cyropaedia,* written in 370 BCE, contains several elements of the novel. Bakhtin finds that the narrative began as an attempt to represent Xenophon's contemporary reality. The heroic past depicted in the narrative is not the national past, and is inspired by an interest in the Orient. This suggests that the world had opened up and moved beyond the closed world of the epic. Cultural interaction between separate languages is evidenced by the representation of the theme of the individual's upbringing, which was to become a major theme in the European novel subsequently. When the present becomes the vantage point of narration, human orientation changes, as is seen in the book. The narrative enters historical time, as becoming, as the inconclusive process of the present comes to be examined. What characterises the novel is the incompleteness of the world in the making. Bakhtin feels that modernity of the novel lies 'in its capacity for re-thinking and re-evaluating' (39).

Equally remarkable is the novel's ability to assimilate non-literary materials such as letters, diaries, confessions, pamphlets and courtly materials. This relationship with extraliterary genres, genres of everyday life and ideological genres gives it a new temporal orientation. The ability to absorb and deploy such historically significant material is characteristic of a developing genre. This also creates a new relationship between the author and the hero. In highly developed classical genres such as the epic and tragedy, the central character is already fully developed. He/She is a completed being. There is nothing more we can add to the epic hero's story both in terms of his/her inner world and external possibilities. Once the epic distance was erased and the image of the individual was transferred to the everyday world of inconclusive events, individuals could no longer be contained by the plots of the new literary works. The heroes in serio-comic genres of antiquity, such as those of Rabelais and Cervantes, wear masks, live unpredictable lives, assume new roles in new plots and project inexhaustible possibilities. Bakhtin writes that they have a 'happy surplus of their own, their own rudimentary but inexhaustible human face' (52). While heroes of epics and tragedies perish, these characters are repeatedly reborn.

In a novel, the hero is not exhausted by the plot. This means that his/her humanness can evolve in new directions, challenging the limits of fate and situation. The hero does not coincide with his/her fate and situation. The author's ideological vision of life and society decides how the surplus humanness in the hero is finally realised. The future remains a perpetual possibility as the hero retains his/her unrealised potential. In Bakhtin's memorable words, 'All existing clothes are always too tight and thus comical on a man' (53). In the epic, the external individual coincides with the inner individual, thus creating the figure of an integrated 'whole' individual. In the novel, this wholeness is fragmented and as a result, the individual has the potential to remake himself/herself.

THE PREHISTORY OF NOVELISTIC DISCOURSE

Bakhtin's 'From the Prehistory of Novelistic Discourse' traces the long history of novelistic discourses in Europe. The novel did not suddenly emerge out of nowhere. It has a long history that goes back to folk sources in many European languages. Critics of the novel, particularly those who applied stylistic approaches to the study of the novel in the second half of the nineteenth century, were unaware of the long prehistory of novelistic genres. Consequently, they read the novel from the perspective of the author. The author's words, metaphors and images were taken to be central to the study of the novel. There were attempts to examine the linguistic aspects of the novelist's language. Descriptions such as the Romantic novel, the Naturalistic novel and the Impressionist novel reduced the entire genre to a particular movement. The language of the novel was often seen as the individual style of a given novelist. All these approaches are reductive as they do not evaluate the specific conditions under which the word lives in the novel. Central to Bakhtin's concept of the novel is the distinction between poetic genres and novelistic genres.

Parody played a significant role in shaping novelistic genres since ancient times. Parody represents the direct world of another as an object of representation. The parodist borrows a manner of seeing and evaluating the world. Bakhtin observes, 'There never was a single strictly straightforward genre, no single type of direct discourse—artistic, rhetorical, philosophical, religious, ordinary, everyday—that did not have its own parodying and travestying double, its own comic-ironic *contre-partie*' (53).

The satyr play, which followed the tragic trilogy, is a good example of this kind of parodic form. Eminent writers such as Sophocles, Euripides and Aeschylus wrote satyr plays. Aeschylus's *Bone Gatherers* (fourth century BCE) reworks national myths from an ironic point of view, providing a corrective to the high seriousness of the high literary form of tragedy. Even before the satyr plays, there existed diverse parodic-travestying forms performed by mimics, impersonators and comic actors whose work constituted 'a special extra-generic or inter-generic field' (83). They reflected, in all its fullness, the heteroglossia and multiple voices of a given culture and society. The parodic-travestying forms liberated language and imagination from the power of the centripetal forces of culture.

Roman literature came under the influence of multiple languages much earlier. The concluding phase of Hellenism was also characterised by 'other-languagedness'. Bakhtin emphasises the Orient's ancient and complex polyglossia and its influence on the cultures of Greece and Rome. For instance, Lucian's native city of Samosata comprised Syrians who spoke Aramaic, an educated upper class who spoke and wrote in Greek, and officials who conducted business in Latin. The road that passed through the city carried caravans from India to Persia and beyond. The role of polyglossia in shaping novelistic genres has parallels in many parts of the world in subsequent phases of history. The Saturnalia festival of Rome during the Middle Ages is of great significance in this context. The scriptural word in its various forms was subjected to critique by the parodying forms during this phase.

It was during the Renaissance that modern European languages such as French, German and English came into their own. They were born of the laughing, travestying genres of the late Middle Ages. For instance, the literary language of French was created by John Calvin and François Rabelais. Born in the process of parodying the sacred word, these languages had access to a long tradition of parodic-travestying genres in European languages. The French historian Ferdinand Bruno has observed that during the Renaissance, an attempt was made to re-establish Latin in all its classical purity and this ironically resulted in making Latin a dead language. Bakhtin concludes that the novelistic word arose and developed over centuries as part of a cultural struggle between several forms of sociopolitical control over the nature of the word.

CHRONOTOPE

Bakhtin wrote his essay, 'Forms of Time and of the Chronotope in the Novel' in 1937–38, though it was published only in 1975. It first appeared in English in 1981. Right from the time he wrote 'Author and Hero in Aesthetic Activity' (1920–23), Bakhtin had a deep interest in the subject of space. 'Outsideness', for him, was the most important creative element in achieving objectivity. In Dostoevsky, there is hardly any reference to landscapes or interiors or background spaces. All his representations of space are deeply ideological. For instance, the narrow, coffin-like room of Raskolnikov is emblematic of the mental space of the character. What one sees is determined by his/her location in time and space. In certain types of fiction, the location itself may not be of consequence. For instance, '221B Baker Street' serves as the address of Sherlock Holmes, but this is of no consequence to the plot or its development. Chronotopes emerge out of an organic unity of time and space, and are deeply implicated in sociopolitical history.

Bakhtin was deeply influenced by Einstein's theory of relativity which rejected the concept of absolute time and space. In his early works he was also greatly influenced by Kant, who had observed that 'space and time are indispensable forms of any cognition, beginning with elementary perception and representations' (qtd. in *The Dialogic Imagination* 85). The term 'chronotope' is derived from the Greek words *khronos* meaning 'time' and *topos* meaning 'space'. He came to use chronotope as a metaphor to denote the intrinsic connectedness of space and time in literary works. He noticed that chronotopes define genres and generic distinctions. They concretise the materiality of space and time, making the novel culturally specific. The ideological elements of the novel such as its political, social and philosophical ideas become accessible through its chronotopes. Bakhtin observes, 'In the literary artistic chronotope, spatial and temporal indicators are fused into one carefully thought-out, concrete whole. Time, as it were, thickens, takes on flesh, becomes artistically visible; similarly, space becomes charged and responsive to the movements of time, plot and history' (84). What is abstract in the novel's ideology and philosophy is transformed into concrete forms of representation through the use of chronotopes.

In his earlier concepts such as dialogism, heteroglossia and polyglossia, the focus was on language. However, with chronotope, Bakhtin is more concerned with the question of time. Chronotope renders time visible, through concrete metaphors. From the ancient Greek novel to the nineteenth-century realistic novel, novelistic narratives have been able to represent the changing locations of human lives through their unending flux, through chronotopes of various kinds. In his essay, Bakhtin provides an exhaustive typology of chronotopes through their historical development, starting from the Greek novels. Bakhtin's classification is only indicative, not exhaustive. Though he does not spell it out, it is obvious that chronotopes can vary from language to language, culture to culture. As there is much in common between the languages of Europe, he is able to locate a common repository of chronotopes in the history of the European novel.

Bakhtin also provides a critical perspective to evaluate space as it is represented in fictional narratives. For instance, the space represented in a novel may be alien for the hero, which means he/she has no control over it. The hero may not achieve complete mastery over it, as he/she cannot comprehend it completely. At the other extreme, we have native space with which the hero is well acquainted, as it is part of his/her homeland. In terms of evolution of space, one may speak of a static or dynamic chronotope. Bakhtin does not use the term 'dynamic chronotope' but his remarks on a 'static' chronotope imply the presence of a 'dynamic' chronotope. In the Roman novel *The Golden Ass* (second century BCE) by Apuleius, the hero undergoes a series of metamorphoses. Here, the space is static as it is already complete with no possibility of further development. In folktales or in the works of Rabelais, space remains dynamic as it is continuously transformed with the progression of the story. The chronotopes in adventure novels of ordeal or everyday life are alien and static. In idyllic fiction, the chronotope is native and static, while in the fiction of the chivalric type it is alien and static. In the picaresque fiction woven around the figures of the Rogue, the Clown and the Fool, the chronotope is native and static. As mentioned above, in Rabelaisian fiction the chronotope is native and dynamic.

Each chronotope can include a large number of minor chronotopes. They are often interwoven with each other as they form a cluster. For instance, the chronotope of the road is common to many types of fiction. One can see it in *The Golden Ass* as well as in Gogol's *Dead Souls.* The chronotope of encounter may combine with that of the road. It is on the road that all social classes meet and mingle. Heroes of the medieval romance set out on the road for long journeys. Chance encounters are part of the plots in *The Golden Ass* and *Satyricon* (first century BCE). In Gothic novels we come across the chronotope of the castle. The castle has associations with aristocracy, monarchy and feudal lords, and its time is saturated with history. Legends, traditions, architectural designs, weapons, insignia and mysterious events are often associated with the castle. For example, in *Jane Eyre* (1847), one can see the lurking presence of the castle in Rochester's house, but it soon undergoes a transformation as it is burnt down. This is a prelude to Jane's transformation into an assertive, independent woman. *Jane Eyre* has elements of the Gothic novel, but it soon becomes a novel of growing up, a bildungsroman, as the spatio-temporal dimensions assimilate more historical time.

Parlours and salons are central to the fictional works of Stendhal, Dostoevsky and Balzac. The chronotope of the provincial town is common to many novels like *Madame Bovary* (1856). Novels that deal with a crisis and a break, partake of the chronotope of the threshold. In Dostoevsky's novels, we often see doors and entrances as intersections where events take place. The rooms, parlours or inns open out to the roads, bringing in the public square. Bakhtin feels that the chronotope of the public square is a continuation from the ancient biography and autobiography. It survives in the works of Rabelais and Dostoevsky. In the history of novels, with several forms such as the biographical novel, the socio-psychological novel and the family novel marking various stages of evolution, Dostoevsky brings out a basic shift in orientation. The hero and his/her world are combined in an organic whole in the biographical novel. Dostoevsky has no use for biographical time, as his heroes are always in a state of becoming, perpetually incomplete. They exist in a time of crisis. They grapple with universal issues of existence and salvation. This is where one can find echoes of Menippean satires in Dostoevsky. We have observed that the carnivalesque character of the public square makes it a basic constituent of the Rabelaisian chronotope. For Dostoevsky, the public square becomes the setting for staging confessions, altercations, even repentance. In Rabelais, it is the place where the high and the low, the sublime and the gross intermingle, ensuring the continuity of life.

Bakhtin discusses at length the idyllic chronotope which extends from ancient times to the present. The love idyll which exists as the pastoral, the idyll that focusses on agricultural labour and the family idyll are some of the types he discusses in detail. Even in modern novels, the landscape of mountains, valleys, fields, rivers and forests make their appearance in various thematic clusters. Such occasions gesture towards another order of reality, far removed from money-centric, predatory capitalism. Bakhtin observes that the destruction of the idyll becomes one of the major themes of literature towards the end of the eighteenth century and in the first half of the nineteenth century. As the idyllic world proved inadequate for the capitalist world, it got demolished and replaced by the chronotope of the bildungsroman. Often, the character bearing the stamp of 'a man of the people' in many modern novels is of idyllic descent as he carries the wisdom of the common folk.

The bildungsroman as a genre heralds the logical completion of the development of the novel over centuries. Several genres such as the travel novel, the novel of ordeal and the biographical or confessional novel have preceded it. These subgenres have been assimilated into the very structure of the bildungsroman. Thus, the picaresque novel, the baroque novel, chivalric romances, hagiographies of saints and martyrs, *Confessions* of Saint Augustine, and the novels of Defoe and Fielding have all contributed towards the emergence of a genre like the bildungsroman. In the novel of ordeal, the hero is the focus, and the external world provides only a setting. In the biographical novel, the space becomes more realistic and detailed.

The bildungsroman embodies the hero's emergence into a new self, which is embodied in the space around him/her. A bildungsroman is primarily a novel of formation, upbringing, education and experience. In the second chapter of his book *Speech Genres and Other Late Essays* (1979), Bakhtin discusses the nature and development of the bildungsroman in great detail. He identifies five different types of novels under the category 'bildungsroman'. In the first type, the time depicted is cyclical, moving from childhood through youth and maturity to old age. These novels tend to be idyllic and present a static world against which the hero moves through various phases in life. In the second type of bildungsroman, life and the world are primarily seen as a school which bestows on the hero experience, maturity and wisdom. The works of Hippel, Jean Paul and Goethe belong to this category.

The third type of bildungsroman is more complex. The emergence of the hero happens in biographical time as he/she goes through stages which are unique and unrepeatable. As a person's character is shaped, his/her destiny is also created along with it. Henry Fielding's *Tom Jones* (1749) and Charles Dickens's *David Copperfield* (1849) are novels of this type, where the hero moves through biographical time to their final destiny. In the fourth type, the didactic dimension of the novel is dominant. Education becomes the central theme as the hero's pedagogical progress is elaborated upon at length, as in Xenophon's *Cyropaedia* and Rousseau's *Emile* (1762). For Bakhtin, the fifth type of bildungsroman represents the final stage of development of this genre. Here, a person's individual emergence is closely linked to the historical emergence of a new order of society. While in the earlier types of bildungsroman, the world was the setting against which the hero evolved and emerged into a new identity, in this fifth category, the world emerges into a new phase, along with the hero. Bakhtin remarks that in novels such as *Gargantua and Pantagruel*, *Simplicius Simplicissimus* (1669) and *Wilhelm Meister's Apprenticeship* (1796), the hero 'emerges *along with the world* and he reflects on the historical emergence of the world itself' (*Speech Genres* 23). This means that the hero is caught between two worlds and epochs. Bakhtin elaborates: 'It is as though the very foundations of the world are changing, and man must change along with them' (23–24).

Implications of the Concept of Chronotope

In the act of narrativisation, fictional techniques are at play. History exists as a narrative and this means that historiography cannot escape the imaginative reconstruction of events to suit certain plots. Hayden White defines 'emplotment' as 'the encodation of the facts contained in the chronicles as specific *kinds* of plot structures' (83). The challenge before the novelist is to impose a form and shape on events which are, by nature, formless and fragmentary.

Time and space are artistically concretised in the chronotope. No event can be understood without reference to their spatial and temporal dimensions. Chronotopes help us organise our experiences into meaningful wholes capable of communicating significance and meaning.

Friedrich Engels's *Dialectics of Nature* (1883) talks of a fundamental break in the history of the world around the fifteenth century. There was a revolution in consciousness which cast every phenomenon, from the cultural to the economic, in a new light. While recognising that there was a rupture in the nature of time around the Renaissance, Bakhtin feels that the significance of time itself has changed since then. The concept of chronotope, as developed by him, implies that human beings need new frames to understand the nature of time, as history undergoes transformation. People of modern times have a fundamentally different concept of time from that of the ancients. Even between the eighteenth and the twenty-first centuries, our cognition of time has changed. Rabelais marks a new attitude towards time because, as Bakhtin argues, 'it was necessary to find a new form of time and a new relationship of time to space' (*The Dialogic Imagination* 206).

Bakhtin has used literary works to map these shifts in conceptual frameworks, but their implications and the relevance of the concept of the chronotope extend beyond literary works. We can conceive of a new era only when we invent new chronotopes to concretise it. Alastair Renfrew argues that one may even consider the Renaissance itself as a chronotope: 'Just as polyglossia—the birth of a multi-languaged consciousness—altered the nature of language and our understanding of it forever, so too time is "altered" in the Renaissance to the point where it may be more justified to regard Renaissance not as a "period" or "a cultural revolution", but rather as a *chronotope*' (123). One may speak of chronotopes of colonialism or late capitalism. Chronotopes help us understand history, the way we comprehend a literary text, as an expression of sociopolitical forces acting on human imagination. This conjunction between literature and history also helps us reinterpret literary history in terms of chronotopes. What is the 'form of time' that is characteristic of a particular epoch in history? Victorian England or postcolonial India has to be understood in terms of specific chronotopes that are internally organic to those societies. Instead of imposing chronotopes borrowed from elsewhere, one should locate chronotopes that help understand the other, in such contexts. Bakhtin's study of author–hero relations and answerability may be instructive here. The embodied subject speaks from his/her own non-iterable location in being. The speaking subject is thus embodied in the chronotope that enables him/her to speak. The question of how historical epochs or events such as colonialism, imperialism and late capitalism shape specific cultures must be viewed through the kind of chronotopes that each of these cultures has given rise to. A novel like *One Hundred Years of Solitude* (1967) reads European colonial history from the perspective of the colonised Colombian subject.

What is magical about the realism of the novel may be located in the way García Márquez 'carnivalises' the chronotopes of the European novel from the historical perspective of Colombia. The people of Macondo go through an epidemic of 'forgetting', which is a unique way of suggesting the relation between colonial authority and the time of the colonised. Postcolonial societies reimagined space–time relations in colonised societies from the position of the radical other. We can deploy Bakhtin's framework to understand the recent developments in the postcolonial novel using the framework he has provided in his essays.

The question of whether the theory of chronotope displaces Bakhtin's central concern with language is also relevant here. If chronotope decides the nature of the narrative, the spoken words of the characters may not be central to the whole question of narrative. In his concluding remarks in 'Forms of Time and of the Chronotope in the Novel', written in 1973, Bakhtin comments on the fundamentally chronotopic nature of language which bears the imprint of space and time: 'Language, as a treasure-house of images, is fundamentally chronotopic. The internal form of the word—the mediating sign through which primary spatial meanings are transferred to temporal relationships (in the broadest sense) is also chronotopic' (252). Bakhtin helps us understand the question of language here from a new perspective: language itself is chronotopic, like a literary genre. In his 'Notes Made in 1970–71', Bakhtin comments on the chronotopicity of artistic thinking: 'A point of view is chronotopic, that is, it includes both the spatial and temporal aspects. The chronotope of the depicted event, the chronotope of the narrator and the chronotope of the author (the ultimate authorial instance)' (*Speech Genres* 134). One can trace time and its movement in language. In his discussions of the great writers such as Goethe and Balzac, Bakhtin comments on their ability to 'see time in space' (*The Dialogic Imagination* 247). Bakhtin considers Goethe the most eloquent representative of the genre of the bildungsroman. The hero of *Wilhelm Meister's Apprenticeship* 'emerges *along with the world* as he reflects the historical emergence of the world itself' (*Speech Genres* 23–24). In *Italian Journey* (1816), Goethe communicates his sense of wonder and excitement after visiting Venice. Venice is no longer a mere word or an empty name for him. Goethe saw everything not from the point of view of eternity, but in time, and in the power of time.

The essential dialectics of the chronotope consist in the relation between *khronos* and *topos:* the former is inexhaustible while the latter gets progressively exhausted. The Renaissance marks a time when geography, or the space of the world, was opened up for exploration. By the Enlightenment, the world was mapped and studied in minute detail. The evolution of genres from the folkloric or mythological to the realistic or geographical, parallels this process. Bakhtin's essays on the novel study this evolution from multiple perspectives. The idea of chronotopes marks an important stage in Bakhtin's conceptual framework, in his quest to study the relation between language and reality.

ETHICS AND AESTHETICS IN BAKHTIN

As a literary theorist, Bakhtin has been primarily concerned with the relations between ethics and aesthetics. This is the unifying thread that runs through his major contributions as a critic, thinker, philosopher of language and humanist. One of the basic tenets of his thought is that all utterances have an addressee who may be far or near, living or dead, a layman or a scholar. The author, in the first instance, directs his/her utterance to such an addressee. But Bakhtin also speaks of a 'super-addressee'. An author also writes for a super-addressee whose 'absolute, just, understanding is presumed' (*Speech Genres* 126) in a distant historical time. According to Bakhtin, in various ages and various understandings of the world, this super-addressee may assume various ideological expressions such as 'God, absolute truth, the court of dispassionate human conscience, the people, the court of history, science and so forth' (126). In *German Ideology* (1867), Karl Marx points out that 'only thought uttered in the word becomes a real thought for another person and only in the same way is it a thought for myself' (62). What Marx says echoes Bakhtin's thought: 'But this other is not only the immediate other (second addressee); the word moves ever forward in search of responsive understanding' (127). This larger significance of Bakhtin's idea of 'addressivity' of utterance has a bearing on the relations between ethics and aesthetics. The word's capacity to address the other enjoins upon the speaking subject the ethical responsibility of 'answerability'.

Why is the novel so central to Bakhtin's thinking? It is here that his ideas find resonance with those of Emmanuel Levinas, Ludvig Wittgenstein, and so on. In his 'Notes Made in 1970–71', Bakhtin observes that in modern times, the high 'proclamatory genres of priests, prophets, preachers, judges, leaders, patriarchal fathers, and so forth' (*Speech Genres* 132) have been replaced by the writer who has no access to a setting or a style. All modern languages have emerged out of the popular and profane genres. The novel emerges from everyday stories, letters, diaries, and so on, as it is a completely secularised genre. The novel arose, expunging the sacred and the authoritarian word. These aspects of the novel, its resistance to the sacrosanct and the official, and its ability to embody the ironical and the antithetical, invest the form with an ethical burden. The word in such a genre lives on the boundary of human relations, ever expanding the possibilities of the social in the world. It is in recasting the issue of the social as a fundamental dimension of language in use, that Bakhtin inscribes the question of the ethical into his theoretical discussions of the literary. It is through the answerable participation effected by a unique act that one gets out of 'the realm of endless draft versions' and rewrites 'one's life once and for all in the form of a fair copy' (*Toward a Philosophy* 44). Here, it is worth remembering that a critic like Walter Benjamin values the experimental 'montage' for its ability to disrupt the habitualised consciousness of modernity. Both Bakhtin and Benjamin were aware of the reifying forces of tradition and constantly explored the spaces shared between the literary, the theological and the philosophical. In his essay on Charles Baudelaire, Benjamin talks of the 'aura' in these words: 'The person we look at, or who feels he is being looked at, looks at us in turn. To perceive the aura of an object we look at means to invest it with the ability to look back' (188). One could explore the deeper relations between Benjamin and Bakhtin from their conceptual concerns with 'looking back' and answerability.

Literature is able to interpret the human situation. For instance, the novel as a literary genre is able to embody, engage with and illuminate human lives as lived in actual surroundings from innumerable perspectives and in the process, transform them into a form that can convey their truth, not in any essentialist manner, but in their complex dialogic relationships. The discursive capaciousness of literature, of the novel in particular, makes it ethical in a fundamental sense. But for literary works, philosophical ideas will never be expressed in concrete situations in all their vividness. In this sense, literature translates ethics into human contexts. Philosophical ideas get concretised in the conflicts of the non-recurrent deeds of subjects who are constituted by the sociopolitical forces of a particular time. Levinas valued the novel in general, and Dostoevsky in particular, for these very reasons.

Wittgenstein has argued that ethics and aesthetics are one. He holds that ethics cannot be expressed in propositional language. Both ethics and aesthetics exceed the propositional limits of language. Ethics is concerned with ultimate questions, but questions of good and evil cannot be expressed in referential language. It can only be articulated through style which, according to Wittgenstein, exceeds propositional language. Style embodies transcendence. Wittgenstein held that the meaning of a word is determined by its use in language. We can arrive at the meaning only by travelling with the word through its meanderings through history. Further, he felt that it is the 'forms of life' that enable language to function and so they should be accepted as a given. Forms of life reflect the flux of life, the contingent nature of life itself. Bakhtin's main concepts address this dimension of language, as he constantly talked about 'outsideness' and boundaries. This is not to imply any parallels between Wittgenstein and Bakhtin, but rather to suggest that the complex relations between language and the world on the one hand, and philosophy, ethics and aesthetics on the other, are a productive area of enquiry for both these thinkers in the twentieth century. Bakhtin would have fully endorsed Wittgenstein's statement that propositional language is unable to communicate value and ideology and also his belief that 'philosophy ought really to be written only as a poetic composition' (58). At a deeper level, they seem to share a belief in the dialogic potential of utterance to address the other, using style which will make use of chronotopes, among other things.

The next chapter will take up the various directions in which Bakhtin Studies have developed over the last few decades, and will also examine Bakhtin's relations with structuralism and poststructuralism. It will explore the question of parallels between Bakhtin, Foucault and Derrida. Bakhtin's works have substantially contributed towards interdisciplinary studies, particularly in the fields of feminism, culture studies (with emphasis on popular culture), and studies of intertextual relations between literature, painting, cinema and stage.

REFERENCES

Bakhtin, Mikhail. *Speech Genres and Other Late Essays*. Trans. Vern W. McGee. Ed. Caryl Emerson and Michael Holquist. 1979. Austin: U of Texas P, 1986. Print.

---. *The Dialogic Imagination: Four Essays.* Trans. Caryl Emerson and Michael Holquist. Ed. Michael Holquist. Austin: U of Texas P, 1981. Print.

Note: The above book contains four important essays: 'Epic and Novel' (3–40), 'From the Prehistory of Novelistic Discourse' (41–83), 'Forms of Time and the Chronotope in the Novel' (84–258) and 'Discourse in the Novel' (259–422). The last essay deserves special mention as it contains Bakhtin's thoughts on the form of the novel in their most distilled form. Unless otherwise mentioned, all references to these essays in the above chapter are provided by page numbers only.

---. *Toward a Philosophy of the Act.* Trans. Vadim Liapunov. Ed. Vadim Liapunov and Michael Holquist. Austin: U of Texas P, 1993. Print.

Benjamin, Walter. *Illuminations.* New York: Schocken Books, 2007. Print.

Marx, Karl, and Friedrich Engels. *German Ideology.* Moscow: Progress Publishers, 1964. Print.

Renfrew, Alastair. *Mikhail Bakhtin.* London and New York: Routledge, 2015. Print.

White, Hayden. 'The Historical Text as Literary Artifact.' *The Norton Anthology of Theory and Criticism*. Ed. Vincent B. Leitch. 1985. New York: W. W. Norton & Company, 2001. Print.

Wittgenstein, Ludwig. *Culture and Value.* Chicago: U of Chicago P, 1980. Print.

Chapter Seven

Bakhtin and Beyond

IMPLICATIONS OF BAKHTIN'S THEORIES AND CONCEPTS FOR HUMANITIES AND LITERARY THEORY

Bakhtin's ideas have implications for humanities in general. It has not been sufficiently recognised that his concepts of dialogism, polyphony, heteroglossia, carnival, chronotope and polyglossia have provided a new critical lexicon for culture studies (for the study of popular culture, in particular), literary criticism and the exploration of intertextual relations between works of art across various genres. As Bakhtin's ideas gained wider currency in the second half of the twentieth century, they were assimilated into the discourses of several other disciplines. He stands at the intersection of multiple disciplines as a transitional figure of interdisciplinarity, helping us recover dimensions of the collective and the social which were muted by the political domination of monologic discourses. Reader–response theory, reception theory, speech act theory and intertextuality are some of the areas where Bakhtinian concepts find resonance. They help recover a perspective of culture rooted in the everyday experience of our times.

Bakhtin's reception was mediated by the poststructuralist critique of the prevailing notions of text, history, self, other, power and resistance. Bakhtin's concepts found favour with several critics who contested formalist and structuralist approaches to society and culture. He is a transitional figure at the conjunction of structuralism and poststructuralism, as his specific object of enquiry is 'the interrelationship between socially and historically grounded languages' (Dentith 88). Bakhtin's rejection of individualism and essentialism brings him closer to Foucault and Derrida, though there are major differences in the nature and objectives of their enquiries. His affirmation that language constitutes the world we inhabit, is echoed by several poststructuralists. The object of knowledge is discursively constituted and cannot be known outside its discursive frame. As Robert Young observes, for both Foucault and Bakhtin, 'society consists of competing contradictory discourses . . . each of which expresses a different order of things that successively strive for and resist totalization' (57). Bakhtin views power in terms of a struggle between centripetal and centrifugal forces which get enacted in the heteroglot structure of society. For Foucault, power breeds resistance and it is the interdependence of power and resistance that defines the dynamics of social organisations. All these formulations have shaped the critical approaches of colonial discourse theory, and subaltern and minority studies. One of the early attempts to examine language as discourse can be seen in Roland Barthes's *S/Z* (1970), which analyses in great detail the codes that inform a fictional text. Each code has its roots in a separate discourse; a text is braided through its interrelations with many other texts. Such an exegesis follows the larger premise that utterances are socially grounded and are value loaded.

Bakhtin's insights into the nature of heteroglossia in human communities have implications beyond the linguistic organisation of society. Language, as a site of conflict, reflects the stratified and fragmented nature of power structures in society. The fissures in social landscape along the lines of class, race, caste and gender assume material forms in the conflicting reality of dialects, minority languages, professional registers, generational divergences in the use of languages, paradoxical meanings and opposing values. No unitary political subject can be conceived of as the foundation of values in the sociopolitical domain. The socio-ideological aspects of languages help us map oppressive regimes of domination and the resistance it breeds. This finds application in minority studies, Black studies and subaltern studies. Gender does not figure directly in Bakhtin's theories, but in studies of the carnival he examines patriarchal authorities and the way desire and carnal passions portray questions of resistance and defiance.

Bakhtin never confined himself to the field of the literary. He was acutely aware of the relation between art and life, literature and society, and the spoken and written word as the embodied act of a living subject. His use of the term 'speech genres' is a case in point, as it carries his stamp of theoretical insight. He speaks of 'primary' speech genres which are rooted in everyday life. For instance, greetings, drunken talk, sermons at a church, lovers talking to each other, jokes, anecdotes, exchanges between people at a market, all these point to real-life contexts where speech enacts an event, creating a bond between multiple selves, between the self and the other. There are written forms such as diaries, letters, pamphlets, advertisements, almanacs, devotional writings and religious discourses which find their way into literary works like the novel. The specialised registers of a lawyer, a doctor, a financial consultant or an engineer also circulate in society in their own particular contexts. Their appearance in a fictional text is modified by the context in which it appears.

Thus, everyday life is made up of endless speech genres which inform and enable our communication. A work of art is an utterance directed at an audience; but at a deeper level, it is woven out of many primary discursive moments from real life. Both its inner orientation and external reception are defined by real-life situations of interrelations between the audience and the author. A work's reception in a society is determined by the real-life situations of a specific time and place. Medvedev/Bakhtin observes, 'Social intercourse is the medium in which the ideological phenomenon first acquires its specific existence, its ideological meaning, its semiotic nature' (qtd. in Morris 127). Genres such as the epic and lyric, as well as dramatic genres, participate in the twin dynamics of production and reception: of being shaped out of the discourses in circulation in society and participating in the real-life conditions of the society in which they circulate.

Before Bakhtin, genres were understood in terms of their internal configuration and stylistic features. However, Bakhtin emphasises how generic conventions and the linguistic aspects of utterance are implicated in the sociopolitical life of the community. Different genres have different ways of shaping and finalising the materials they take from life. The immediate conditions of performance and perception determine the 'meaning' of a work of art. There are generic attributes that determine the reception, but conditions of reception shape its content and meaning. This is where the dialogic dimension of utterance becomes central. All utterances anticipate a response and this process is part of a historical process of meaning-making.

Form, for Bakhtin, is not a question of compositional characteristics, such as the use of iambic pentameter or blank verse. What is of greater importance is the function they perform in relation to the architectonics of the event of the literary work. The production of meaning is not a matter of the author's intention alone. It is met with other utterances in the surroundings of the text. Polysemy is not inherent in writing; it issues from the relationship between writing and the reader. This is where the role of the reader becomes central. Critics of the schools of reception and reader–response theories have meticulously analysed these aspects of textual reproduction through the ages from multiple perspectives.

Bakhtin has been critical of stylistics as a discipline because in the novel, the word of the author is not final. The author's discourse does not exhaust the discourses of characters. In the novel, a diversity of 'social speech types are artistically organized' ('Discourse in the Novel' 262). What is often mistaken as style is the direct speech of the author. In a society where the novel takes centre stage, all other genres come under its influence. Novelisation is thus a cultural phenomenon one witnesses from the nineteenth century onwards, across languages. Bakhtin argues that as genres become more dialogic, they get novelised. Bakhtin's overemphasis on the idea of the novel as the most evolved form, the only form capable of embodying fluid reality in its moment of emergence, makes his theory of genres singular and different from that of writers like Northrop Frye. This has implications for pedagogy as well as literary research. Critical writings on the novel tend to focus on themes and style, leaving out questions of form altogether. While it is easier to come to terms with questions of form in a lyric or a drama, a long narrative like *Ulysses* (1920) or *Crime and Punishment* (1866) may not be available for formal analysis unless one is equipped with a critical vocabulary which can access the way the novel functions as an utterance. Bakhtin provides an exhaustive analysis of chronotopes that appear in various kinds of novels, which enables one to see how a new novel carries within its formal structure 'generic memories' of its origin.

INTERTEXTUALITY

In post-1970 literary criticism, the cultural turn marks an important shift in both the humanities and the social sciences. At the core of this shift is a perception of the inherent monologism of the various disciplines which were conceived in the heyday of colonialism and imperialism. The liberal democratic consensus had posited a universal subject as the normative arbitrator of all meanings. As this edifice of modernity came crashing down, Bakhtin's ideas of heteroglossia and polyphony opened up new ways of engaging the other. For Bakhtin, novelisation was a process that contested canonisation of all kinds. The division of culture into 'high' and 'low' implies a stratified, hierarchical society. Bakhtin reconceived the very ideas of genre, text and literature through his concepts of utterance, heteroglossia and polyphony. He held that 'a genre lives in the present, but always remembers its past, its beginning' (*Problems of* 106). The ability of the genre to remain contemporary in every age reinforces the idea of intertextuality. The concept of 'generic memory' helps one see how texts within a genre speak to each other. Julia Kristeva has abstracted the idea of intertextuality without reference to the larger framework of genres and their ability to speak to one another: 'Any text is constructed as a mosaic of quotations; any text is the absorption and transformation of another. The notion of *intertextuality* replaces that of inter-subjectivity' (66).

To say that all texts echo each other, or that every text is woven out of several other texts, would be a false interpretation of the Bakhtinian notions of intertextuality. Bakhtin does not reject the referential semantic context and content of texts. The postmodern idea of signifiers endlessly circulating in their own orbits with no source or destination, with no centre or circumference, does not do justice to Bakhtin's philosophical system.

Bakhtin understood that the prevailing approach to genres did not allow any innovation; there was no way one could accommodate emergent genres within the system. As Derrida observed in 'The Law of Genre' (1980), genre implied a limit and its implications were often negative; it meant 'Do Not' (203). Derrida also shows how Maurice Blanchot 'had often had occasion to modify the genre-designation from one version of his work to the next or from one edition to the next' (214). Friedrich Schlegel argued that every poem is a genre in itself. It is necessary to evaluate Bakhtin's consistent concern with genres and speech genres as a recurring theme in European poetics and philosophy.

Enabled by Bakhtin's insights, Kristeva moved from the formal properties of genres to the signifying practices that sustain and distinguish them. Texts absorb and transform each other. Kristeva's theory of intertextuality helps one conceive of certain aspects of textuality from the perspective of the intersection of texts. However, Bakhtin remains more radical in his theory of genres, as he conceives of genres being basic to human communication. Each period and each social group has its repertoire of speech forms for ideological communication. It is this concern with the social and political dimensions of speech genres that sets Bakhtin apart. His emphasis on 'voice' is largely lost in Kristeva's critical elaboration: 'I hear voices in everything and dialogic relations among them' (*Speech Genres* 169). Distinct speech genres have 'specific points of views, specific approaches, forms of thinking, nuances and accents characteristic of the given genre' ('Discourse in the Novel' 289). Bakhtin approaches genres from the perspective of their ability to assimilate history. Genres do not remain the same, as they are both historical and transhistorical. For him, the novel remains the most democratic, dynamic, creative and open-ended genre, which leaves genres like poetry and drama far behind.

Bakhtin had set out to revise the traditional theory of genres, and in the process, he demolished the foundations of a poetics rooted in the opposition between poetry and drama. Kristeva was fascinated by Bakhtin's concept of the word as a domain in which discourses confront each other. It was the political dimension of Bakhtin's 'sociological poetics' that she chose to build on. She drew on Bakhtin's critical works on Dostoevsky and Rabelais to formulate her propositions. The distinction she made between the 'semiotic' and 'symbolic' aspects of language are derived from Bakhtin's insights into utterance, dialogism and polyphony. For Kristeva, the semiotic and symbolic aspects of language are interdependent, but they pull in opposite directions. The semiotic implies the impulsive, the poetic and the maternal, which subverts the rule-governed grammatical aspects of the language. The semiotic breaches the oppressive aspects of the language, as in the polyphonic or the carnivalesque. For Bakhtin, the dialogic resides more at the semantic level, whereas for Kristeva it extends to the syntactic and phonic levels. For both Bakhtin and Kristeva, texts look towards the future, they are unfinalisable. This enables the subject-in-process to be represented within the text. Texts do not remain fixed in their points of origin; they accommodate new contexts and assume new significance for a new audience. This process can only be understood through intertextual relations over an extended period.

In his 1971 essay 'From Work to Text', Barthes visualised the text as something that is experienced only as an activity of production. Barthes's essay echoes Bakhtin and Kristeva's works in several ways, though he does not acknowledge their works directly. For Barthes, a text has no closure and comes without the inscription of the Father. These are elements Bakhtin elaborates on in a different language in his work on polyphony and carnival. Bakhtin had underlined the fact that all living discourses, literary or otherwise, enter 'the dialogically agitated and tension-filled environment of alien words, value judgements and actions' ('Discourse in the Novel' 276). In this sense, all textuality is intertextuality. The idea of an 'inter-text', which marks the intersection of many texts, is productive to the discussion of several literary works. For instance, how can we read *Wide Sargasso Sea* (1966) as a re-writing of *Jane Eyre* (1847)? The original novel, which was a Victorian classic, used the figure of the Caribbean woman as the other to bestow on Jane the gift of self-independence. In rewriting Jane's story of growing up from the perspective of the mad woman in the attic, Jean Rhys produces a critique of imperialism as patriarchal and oppressive. The novel exists as an intertext which echoes and relocates the earlier narrative in another history, with an ideological orientation that is critical and liberating.

BAKHTIN AND POPULAR CULTURE

In the last few decades, there has been a greater interest in popular culture. Bakhtin has contributed towards the understanding of popular culture through his study of the folkloric roots of carnival culture. In contemporary society, it is possible to identify a parallel world of 'underground' literature that questions the official worldview. Through blogs, graphic novels, caricatures, parodies, trolls, pastiches, comic strips and stand-up comedies, the modes of 'high' expression in literature, philosophical thought, academic writing, political commentary and mainstream public opinions are exposed and subjected to ridicule. At the root of these articulations, one can find the double-voiced discourse from the margins of society. Colloquialisms, ellipses, fantasies, archaic idioms, street songs and anecdotes are now being studied in detail to identify their dialogic orientations.

Carnival as a category has been highly productive, finding its application in studies of popular culture, cinema, theatre, fiction and poetry. It contests asymmetries of various kinds, from class, caste and gender to canons and genres. Carnival forms have always used the mask of the mad man, the fool or the *vidushak*. The tragic world of *King Lear* is brought down from its sublime heights to the everyday world of gross emotions through the interventions of the fool. Falstaff is a character that has its roots in the carnival culture of the public square. The 'high' values of aristocracy and royalty are turned upside down by Falstaff through his acts of profanity. Hysteria, as articulated in women's texts, has been traced to carnival culture. The semiotic dimensions of language mentioned by Kristeva use the primitive and the transgressive. In a novel like *Beloved* (1987) by Toni Morrison, we find her language breaking down into fragments, invoking the collective unconscious as Denver returns to the novel as a ghost. The repressed history of the Black community can enter the direct word of the fiction writer only as the other. The popular culture of the Black community enables Morrison to discover the resources for articulating the history of their silence and the violence they endured.

In a modern Indian English novel like *Midnight's Children* (1981), it is possible to discern intertextual elements which question the linear world of English. This is one of the few novels where history, double-voiced discourse and grotesque realism associated with dialogism and carnival have been deployed with telling effect. Right from his birth at the stroke of midnight when India gained independence, Salim Sinai's life becomes a theatre of unpredictable events which turn his life into an allegory of India's history after independence. Rushdie deviates from the standard syntax of English, imparting it intertextual resonances with Urdu and Hindi. Long-winded sentences meander through many subclauses to bring together multiple levels of reality, making the narrative an ever-changing kaleidoscope of the social and political events of north India. At birth, he was exchanged by the midwife, Mary Pereira, and thus became the son of Ahmad and Amina Sinai. He becomes the son of many mothers and fathers. At one point, he says, 'Giving birth to parents has been one of my strange talents' (243). 'Hand-cuffed to history' at birth, all major events in modern Indian history parallel his personal life in the most unexpected ways.

Salim Sinai's face itself becomes a mask in Rushdie's descriptions: 'large moon face was too large'; 'something was lacking in the region of the chin'; 'dark stains spread down my western hairline'; 'a dark patch covered my eastern ear'; 'temples like stunted horns' (124). The fragmented and asymmetrical appearance signifies a dimension of history he personifies. All this turns Salim into a carnivalesque figure. This effect is deepened by his double-voiced manner of speaking. Rushdie uses the orality of Indianisms both in the choice of words and syntax, as seen in the following sentence: 'I am tearing myself apart, can't even agree with myself, talking arguing like a wild fellow, cracking up, memory going, yes, memory plunging into chasms and being swallowed by the dark, only fragments remain, none of it makes sense anymore!' (343). As in the epics, Salim Sinai's birth and life have been foretold by an astrologer.

Ram Seth tells his mother: 'A son, Sahiba, who will never be older than his motherland—neither older nor younger. . . . There will be two heads—but you shall see only one—there will be knees and a nose, a nose and knees. . . . Newspaper praises him, two mothers raise him!' (87). One can work out the intertextual features of the narrative at every point in great detail and also examine the elements that contribute to the grotesque realism of the narrative.

CHRONOTOPES IN INDIAN FICTION

It is possible to extend the above typology to Indian fiction and comment on certain features. The Indian village has been a major chronotope in the social realist tradition of Indian languages. Premchand's *Godan* (1936), Rabindranath Tagore's *Ghare baire* (1916) and Raja Rao's *Kanthapura* (1938) are chronicles of life lived in a village community. Though there are vast differences in their plots, the binary of the village and the town/city figures in these novels as a site of conflict between different ideologies and points of views. In Hindi, there has been a tradition of *anchalik* (regional) novels which deal with a specific region. Phanishwar Nath Renu's *Maila anchal* (1954) is a classic in this category as it deals with the changing life and times in a remote village in Bihar, near the Nepal border, during the turbulence of the Quit India movement. The well-known Marathi novel *Garambicha bapu* (1952) by Shripad Narayan Pendse is set in a village in Konkan called Garambi. In all these novels, the village comes across as a dynamic and native chronotope which is in flux. It is important to note that a village or a region is not a verifiable physical location but an ideological construct woven from collective memory, emotional bonds, conflicts resulting from sociopolitical differences and the anxieties of belonging, all of which are filtered through the prism of an author's vision. It transgresses the limits of the given through its creative invocation of the beyond.

Maila anchal illustrates the polyglossia and heteroglossia that stage the local and the regional. What is represented is a set of relationships that can only be delineated through layered descriptions of lives lived. The novel is set in Maryganj, in the Purnea district of Bihar, which adjoins Bengal on one side and Nepal on the other. The characters in the novel speak Maithili, Bhojpuri, Magahi, Nepali, Bengali and Santhali, not to mention English. This polyglossia creates a dense narrative where multiple voices from different strata of society are heard. The heteroglossia of this society is realised in the plurality of discourses in the novel. We hear the standard Hindi of the educated middle class and the dialects of the rustic characters. It also includes *bhajans*, *kirtans*, songs, sayings and anecdotes from everyday life. While Doctor Prashant or the Tehsildar speaks standard Hindi, the rural characters speak in their respective dialects which depend on their caste, social class and educational background. What makes this novel an exceptional work of art is the way its narrative performs the heteroglossia of the society it depicts. As the values of the zamindari system come to be questioned by the emergent socialist ideology, the conflicts in the novel reflect the internal contradictions of an India in transition. The novel deals with the turbulent years of 1946–48 when India gained its freedom, Gandhi was assassinated and the zamindari system was abolished. Heteroglossia and polyglossia represented in the novel enact the fault lines that characterise Indian rural society at a critical junction in modern history. The dialogism of the narrative alerts us to the multiple polarities that define Indian society.

DIALOGIC IMAGINATION IN THREE MODERN INDIAN NOVELS

In the rest of the chapter, we shall examine three Indian novels which have acquired iconic status in Indian fiction: O. V. Vijayan's *Khasakkinte ithihasam* (originally published in Malayalam in 1968; published in English as *The Legends of Khasak* in 1992), U. R. Ananthamurthy's *Samskara* (originally published in Kannada in 1965; translated by A. K. Ramanujan in 1978), and Bhalchandra Nemade's *Kosla* (originally published in Marathi in 1968; translated by Sudhakar Marathe and published as *Cocoon* in 1997). These novels enact the crisis of modernity that a postcolonial society goes through. It is the way the narrative of these novels embodies this crisis that makes them different. In *The Legends of Khasak*, Khasak is a village on the border of Kerala and Tamil Nadu, near Palghat, where Ravi, a restless, solitary young man with an inquisitive mind, immerses himself in the archaic charms of its age-old beliefs and customs. Praneshacharya of *Samskara*, who had always led a priest's ascetic life in pursuit of brahminic dharma, was not prepared for the crisis that shook the very foundations of his knowledge and practices. In *Cocoon*, Pandurang Sangvikar's coming of age brings up several critical lessons about the moral decline of the Maharashtrian middle class. Through the alienated figures of Ravi, Praneshacharya and Sangvikar, located in their separate social and cultural narratives, these novels enact a series of dialogic encounters between the self and the other, tradition and modernity, the individual and the community, caste and sexuality, and emancipatory ideals and capitalist values. Heteroglossia, polyphony, plurality of voices, chronotopes of journey, encounters, liminal moments on the threshold and the subject-in-process in the flux of sociocultural transitions are basic to the formal enactment of the social critique of Indian modernity presented in these three novels.

The Legends of Khasak succeeds in embodying the subculture of the rustic characters of the village of Khasak. Vijayan's own English translation does not communicate the polyphony of voices we find in the original narrative. When the villagers discuss various viewpoints regarding the new school, in the original, they conclude: 'Truths are many'. However, in Vijayan's self-translation, this becomes: 'Many truths make the big truth' (36). In the original, there are the ravuthars and ezhavas, the local castes, but in the English translation they become 'the Muslims and the Hindus' (11). The creative turbulence of self-doubts and scepticism that produced the polyphonic structure of the original work was replaced by dogmatic faith in the English translation. The dialects spoken in Khasak are emblematic of the religious and caste divisions in the village. They carry resonances of oral cultures that have deep roots in folk culture. The voice of the author in the novel is represented through the hero, Ravi, who speaks in standard Malayalam. What makes the novel a meditation on the complex nature of modernity in twentieth-century Kerala, is the clash between the ideological burden of the multiple discourses Vijayan is able to represent in the context of devaluation of idealistic and emancipatory ideologies. Each of these discourses carries a different evaluative point of view and cannot be contained and circumscribed by the hero's point of view. For instance, Nizam Ali is a critical insider whose alienation is radically different from that of Ravi, whose scepticism confines him to a blind alley. Appukkili, the mentally challenged boy who is claimed by both religious factions in the village, is a liminal figure, problematising normative concepts of reason/unreason, human/subhuman and worldly/other-worldly. In that sense, each of the characters has an evaluative function in the ideological landscape of the novel, where the local is a site of many such contestations and conflicts.

Praneshacharya, in U. R. Ananthamurthy's *Samskara,* is given to a life of rituals and penance as prescribed by the shastras. He also takes care of his physically challenged wife. Narayanappa, a rebel, has lived a wayward life given to carnal pleasures. He suddenly dies of fever, and the brahmin community is caught in a moral crisis regarding his funeral. According to some, he does not deserve to be cremated according to brahmin customs, as he has always been an outsider to their system. Praneshacharya is unable to decide, as the dead body lies unburied. Meanwhile, a plague breaks out in the village. His sexual encounter with Chandri, who belongs to a lower caste and is Narayanappa's mistress, changes the direction of his life. Now Praneshacharya is no different from Narayanappa and his allegiance to brahminic values is under stress. From the sheltered world of exclusivist values, he is thrown into the outside world where his ideological moorings are lost. Putta, a simpleton, tags along with him and they both run into harrowing experiences which deepen his sense of isolation and alienation. Having lost his faith in traditional brahminism, he is unable to shape a new identity to suit the flux of his experience. At the end of the novel, we see him suspended between a past that is closed and a future which is uncertain. He may return to his village a changed man, whose sense of belonging will never be the same.

Praneshacharya's complete surrender to the brahminic code of dharma, renders his world static and closed. His sexual union with Chandri marks a fall from grace, but this involves a discovery of Narayanappa's demonic force as a part of his own inner self. The novel shifts towards the chronotope of the threshold as Praneshacharya's world slowly falls apart. It moves towards a crisis as the brahminic world confronts questions of critical choices in a secular world. There are no answers in the shastras for the problem at hand, and this opens up a world of self-doubt and self-enquiry. The novel becomes dialogic in its depiction of Praneshacharya's moral crisis, as the monologic self-sufficiency of brahminic faith cannot sustain itself. He is not able to accuse Narayanappa as a sinner, as he is also implicated in the same transgression. In becoming his own other, Praneshacharya is now a split self, pulled in different directions.

The chronotope of the threshold appears in Dostoevsky when the hero is caught in a moral crisis. In such a novel, there is a sudden dislocation in the course of events. Praneshacharya's belief system is shaken after a series of chance encounters which constitute another important chronotope in the novel. The sexual encounter with Chandri, which completely alters his life, is a significant chronotope. This happens in the forest, which carries associations of mystery and mysticism in Indian fiction. In many nineteenth-century Indian novels, one comes across forest temples which become the setting for the other-worldly and the transcendental.

As Praneshacharya sets out on his journey with Putta, we are in the familiar territory of historical time as implied by the chronotope of the road. Putta is a combination of the clown and the trickster, providing an idyllic edge to the narrative. He is a drifter and has no commitment to any ideology. In his translation, A. K. Ramanujan writes, 'Putta is a denizen of the world—he is so thoughtlessly one with the world that he is a marvel' (142). In the first part of the novel, we find time standing still as the *agrahara* is an insular space suspended in time, with no relation to historical time. However, as the novel develops, Praneshacharya is thrown into the social world of various castes and creeds, where he has no privileges and his social status becomes ambiguous. This is how the novel assimilates historical time. The chronotope of the road transforms the temporal–spatial dimensions of the novel. Bakhtin has noted that within a single novel, one may notice a number of different chronotopes and complex interactions among them. It is the interrelationships between multiple chronotopes that should be of particular interest in the study of novels.

What makes *Samskara* dialogic is its enactment of the clash between multiple ideologies through its characters. The *agrahara* is a chronotope that indicates a closed world of traditional hegemonic values. Once Praneshacharya moves out of his *agrahara*, his ethical evaluation of reality takes on a different colour. Money, carnal desire, violent competition to dominate and conquer, and use of material power to overpower others are characteristic of the secular world order he is cast into. The carnivalised spectacles of street scenes and Putta's incessant chatter that adds to Praneshacharya's moral anxiety, become modes of representing a new moral evaluation of the ideological plane. The spatial dimensions are not mere settings, but are integral to the deepening moral crisis at the centre of the novel. The novelist represents a world of conflicting points of view, where neither the hero nor the other has absolute control over the ideological plane. The novel ends in an ambivalent stasis, where the hero is stranded between a world he no more holds as authentic and a new world he is not able to completely identify with. The open-ended narrative points to a shift in the order of values and continuing engagements with the subject as an emergent process. Here, it may be noted that the modernist Indian novel is characterised by the alienated hero's ambivalent relation to the outer world. Heroes like Ravi and Praneshacharya render visible subliminal sociopolitical processes which can only be embodied through speech genres of a society located in a specific time and place.

Pandurang Sangvikar is the main character in *Kosla.* Sangvi is a village in the Khandesh region of Maharashtra. Pandurang's father is a rich farmer of the village, and his childhood is spent in the shadow of his father's disciplinarian ways. The first section deals with his unpleasant childhood and his relations with family members. He moves out of the village to pursue studies at a college in Pune. The second and third sections describe his life at the college for the next four years. He drifts away from his family during this time, with his father's menacing figure lurking in the background. Pandurang fails his BA examination and is haunted by a sense of failure. He stays on in Pune to repeat his examination and feels lonely and lost in the big city. Finally, he goes back to his village, with nothing to show to the world after spending years in Pune. The last two sections deal with his life in the village, alienated from his family and community, in search of questions he is not equipped to answer.

Kosla uses the chronotope of the bildungsroman, as it is a narrative about the emergence of the hero. The title, *Kosla*, which means 'cocoon' in Marathi, points to the theme of emergence and transition. His retrospective gaze records those incidents and events that have a bearing on the identity which remains a future possibility, in a life which is ever in flux. It is this unfinalisability that hangs heavy on the protagonist, which is embodied in the voice of the narrative, which is fragmentary and frustrated, creative and critical. His fancies, friendships, failures, all become coloured by the larger theme of the quest for an authentic self in a world which can no longer sustain a belief in egalitarian values, in its complete surrender to materialistic pursuits. The genre of the bildungsroman often portrays the conflict with the father as a central event. Pandurang is unable to accept his father's value system, who values money more than human relations. In his father, he confronts patriarchy in all its menacing oppressiveness for the first time.

Money is a chronotope in the modern Indian novel, as it is deeply implicated in the capitalist economy of consumption and competition. The theme of money is central to novels that deal with the coming of age. Pandurang's father reminds him of the money he spends on him in every letter he sends him. Pandurang was profligate with money and this landed him in trouble. The boys in Pune with their deceptive ways would make him pay for tea and exploit him. Pandurang is quick to notice that behind the urban sophistication lay the same greed and duplicity he had noticed in the village, in his father and others. The same shallowness characterises their sensibilities in literature and the arts. He finds the comic plays that were performed in college, that evoked laugh riots, extremely disturbing.

Pandurang's sensibility is at a formative stage and his confrontation with the duplicity and philistinism that characterised the elite institution in Pune makes him aware of the complexity of his surroundings. Since self-development takes place in relation to the environment of one's own being, Pandurang's self-creation becomes psychologically harrowing. His disillusionment with the 'learned teachers' adds to this state of confusion. He says: 'Truth to tell, the notions I used to have before about the erudition of my teachers proved correct in only one or two cases' (55). His parodies of mainstream Marathi poems add to the motif of carnivalisation in the novel.

As Bakhtin says, in a bildungsroman, the world outside is not a silent background, but is in a state of emergence. The hero's self is intricately related to the world outside. This is true of *Kosla* as well, as Pandurang's struggle is against the values embodied by the Marathi middle-class value system. The middle class of Maharashtra had become self-seeking and consumerist in the post-1947 period. The idea of community implicit in an idealist value system was gradually lost. The individual was the measure of all things. This meant that community values or anything that would benefit society at large had little relevance for the young generation. Pandurang's line of thought shows how he was against setting the literary as an insular domain of sanctity cut off from ordinary life: 'Now I have myself seen many people who are great and yet haven't written a single line. Only fifteen per cent can read and write, so does that mean there is no greatness in the remainder of humanity?' (207). The flow of common life that brings out the contradictions in the ideological positions of intellectuals who live a double life, one at the personal level and the other at the intellectual level, bothers Pandurang. One of the central themes of *Kosla* deals with the process of bringing life and art in consonance with each other.

The hero's suffering and struggle are central to the bildungsroman, as it moves to a moment of self-discovery. One may recall the epiphanies Stephen Dedalus goes through in his journey to becoming a writer in *The Portrait of the Artist as a Young Man* (1916). Pandurang suffers a traumatic loss in the death of his sister, Mani, with whom he was very close. When Mani was ill, his father was busy demolishing their house and rebuilding it. He felt his father had not paid enough attention to her. For days, Pandurang is unable to contain his rage at the death of his sister. He wanders through the streets of Pune at night. The unsettling period of anguish and extreme grief become his initiation into the mystery of death. Perhaps he had never felt such intense pain in all his life. His anger against his insensitive father transforms into an awareness about the vulnerability of life itself. He makes a trip to Ajanta around this time and is deeply moved by the huge sculptures of the Buddha and the paintings on his life and philosophy. A new sensibility is in the making as he is able to perceive the ability of art to aesthetically transform life's distress and disillusionment. His own pain appears trivial in comparison with the burden of pain the Buddha had internalised in his gestures and visage. Pandurang's passage through this traumatic experience amounts to a rite of passage from the innocence of carefree adolescence to a stage of greater maturity. After this, he distances himself from the new house built by his father since it signifies his patriarchal arrogance and insensitivity. He sees it as a tomb built on the dead body of his sister. He feels that the old house was better. His lost childhood spent in open spaces, in the company of people comes back to him. The new house appears to him like a fortress, shutting off people from gaining easy access. When he goes to his new room, he finds it isolated and closed to the outside world. He looks for an opportunity to have a showdown with his father. Finally, he talks back to his father for an hour without pause, addressing him irreverently, and ultimately has to be pulled away by his mother. This completes the break with his father.

Pandurang's emergence as a young man is accompanied by a deepening sense of his alienation from family, village and community. The deception that he experiences at every stage of his journey, from the village to the city, indicates the failure of the moral imagination that underlies the very idea of modernity. In the last two sections of the novel, he points to the resources that may hold out the possibility of such a reimagining. Pandurang is back in his village, having failed his BA examination. His days are given to aimless wanderings and reflections. He reads Mahanubhav literature of the eleventh century and finds a kindred soul in the figure of Chakradhar Swami, who had preached renunciation as a way of discovering oneself. He quotes the following lines from Chakradhar:

> One's own country needs to be forsaken:
> One's own village needs to be forsaken:
> The relation of relations particularly needs to be forsaken. (222).

Pandurang is unable to follow the path of renunciation, caught as he is in moral doubts for which there are no clear answers. His friend Giridhar, who shares his alienation and sense of futility, is at least capable of acting. He chooses to put into practice what he feels is right. Pandurang, on the other hand, feels a sense of ambivalence and void, an inability to believe and belong. He knows it takes courage to say 'no', which is needed to reconstitute oneself. Pandurang's emergence coincides with a sociopolitical stage in India's modern history. The novel acquires allegorical connotations in representing the hero's journey towards a point of self-discovery.

To conclude, Bakhtin has made a difference to the way we think about language, discourse, dialogue, text, orality, genre, popular culture and so on. He was a transitional figure who moved across disciplines, identifying connections and interrogating the essentialist and individualist fallacies rooted in specialised scholarship. He cleared a path to reconfigure humanities from the perspective of the margins and the boundaries. Literature, for him, was deeply implicated in the culture of the entire epoch, as it constitutes an ethically answerable domain of reciprocal relations that excludes nothing that concerns human life. As the discussions of the various literary texts mentioned above will testify, a Bakhtinian mode of reading enables us to position ourselves in the location of the other and view the world from outside. The novel's ability to invoke a moral universe derives from its deep immersion in the everyday social, its power to embody the voices of the meek and the marginalised. The profound possibilities inherent in Bakhtin's conceptual categories may unfold themselves in future when we grasp the nature of the crisis that afflicts humanities today.

REFERENCES

Ananthamurthy, U. R. *Samskara*. Trans. A. K. Ramanujan. Delhi: Oxford UP, 1978. Print.

Bakhtin, Mikhail. 'Discourse in the Novel.' *The Dialogic Imagination: Four Essays*. Trans. Caryl Emerson and Michael Holquist. Ed. Michael Holquist. Austin: U of Texas P, 1981. Print.

---. *Problems of Dostoevsky's Poetics*. Trans. and Ed. Caryl Emerson. Minneapolis: U of Minnesota P, 1984. Print.

---. *Speech Genres and Other Late Essays*. Trans. Vern W. McGee. Ed. Caryl Emerson and Michael Holquist. 1979. Austin: U of Texas P, 1986. Print.

Dentith, Simon, ed. *Bakhtinian Thought: An Introductory Reader*. London, New York: Routledge, 1996. Print.

Derrida, Jacques. 'The Law of Genre.' *Glyph* 7 (Spring, 1980): 1–22. Print.

Duff, David. 'Intertextuality Versus Genre Theory: Bakhtin, Kristeva and the Question of Genre.' *Paragraph* 25.1 (March, 2002): 54–73. Print.

Hoy, Mikita. 'Bakhtin and Popular Culture.' *New Literary History* 23.3 (Summer, 1992): 765–82. Print.

Kristeva, Julia. 'Word, Dialogue and Novel.' *Desire in Language: A Semiotic Approach to Literature and Art*. Trans. Thomas Gora, Alice Jardine and Leon Roudiez. Ed. Leon S. Roudiez. London: Basil Blackwell, 1980. Print.

Morris, Pam, ed. *The Bakhtin Reader: Selected Writings of Bakhtin, Medvedev, Voloshinov*. London: Arnold Publishers, 1994. Print.

Nemade, Bhalchandra. *Cocoon*. Trans. Sudhakar Marathe. Mumbai: Popular Prakashan Pvt. Ltd., 2014. Print.

Rushdie, Salman. *Midnight's Children*. 1981. London: Vintage, 2005. Print.

Vijayan, O. V. *The Legends of Khasak*. New Delhi: Penguin Classics, 1991. Print.

Young, Robert. *Torn Halves: Political Conflict in Literary and Cultural Theory*. Manchester: Manchester UP, 1996. Print.

Glossary of Select Terms

Act: An act may be a word, an utterance or a deed. It cannot be repeated without changing its meaning or significance. Acts are performed by embodied subjects located in a specific time and place. The 'once-occurrent event of Being' can be understood only in terms of deeds, and not abstractions (*Toward a Philosophy* 1).

Addressivity: As a living human being, I have to respond to others' deeds and words. I have no 'alibi' for my existence, which means that my position in the world cannot be substituted by someone else, nor can my responsibility for action be transferred to somebody. I can give meaning and value to my life only by engaging in a dialogue with the world as it exists for me. I am addressed by the world constantly and I should address it in return. It is my responsibility to address the world beyond my immediate contexts. The person whom I address, the addressee, helps me find myself. Every word or utterance has an addressee, though his/her degree of proximity, concreteness and awareness may vary. The person who responds and understands becomes a third party in the dialogue. It is in this sense that Bakhtin says that a word in language is half someone else's. The author or speaker has to seek and surpass the responsive understanding of the addressee. Bakhtin also speaks of a 'super-addressee' whose absolutely just understanding is presumed. Such a super-addressee can assume different ideological expressions depending on the time and place we live in, 'such as God, absolute truth, the court of dispassionate human conscience, the people, the court of history and science and so forth' (*Speech Genres* 126).

Aesthetic Event: The aesthetic event consists of a dialogic interaction between two autonomous consciousnesses. This is different from an 'ethical event', where the two consciousnesses completely merge into each other.

Aesthetic Seeing: Bakhtin uses this term in the context of the inability of abstract theoreticism to grasp 'once-occurrent acts'. Aesthetic seeing suggests an emotional or intuitive orientation towards the other. It can also produce a fragmentary understanding of the object as it fails to ground its emotional response in the position of the 'embodied subject'. It may be a reductive way of grasping an object, by dissolving it in an emotional discourse. In that sense, aesthetic seeing is diametrically opposed to abstract theoreticism. Bakhtin disapproves of the excessive aestheticisation of life he finds in Henri Bergson.

Answerability: My life as an event is accomplished through the participation of others. Another being acquires value and significance for me when I engage with him/her in the outside world. This outside world exists for me through a commitment on my end. What validates life, transforms it into knowledge and understanding *for me*, is an 'answerable consciousness'. Such a consciousness is accountable and responsible for its acts. Social bonds are made possible by this answerability on the part of every self.

Architectonics: Bakhtin had titled his first set of essays *The Architectonics of Answerability* (1990). He was concerned with the relations between parts and the whole in these essays. His primary focus was on self–other relations. The interlocking structures of self–other relations form 'a concrete architectonics of the actual world of performed acts' (*Toward a Philosophy* 54). Values belonging to different domains such as the scientific, aesthetic, religious and political are arranged around the architectonic points of the actual world. It is a fluid and dynamic model where the nature of relations can change.

Author: Bakhtin uses the term 'author' in different senses. It can refer to a real author like Dostoevsky or Rabelais. 'Author' may also imply the creative self of the author as he/she engages with the hero, or with his/her characters. Here, 'author' is a cognitive construct. For Bakhtin, the author–hero relation reflects the self–other relation. The demarcation between author and hero is not absolute, as the self often crosses into the other. One can be the self and also the other. The author comes into being along with the hero. Outside that moment, there is no author. Hence, for Bakhtin, the author is 'the uniquely active form-giving energy that is manifested . . . in a durably valid cultural product' ('Author and Hero' 5).

Being: Bakhtin understands 'being' as 'co-being'. The self needs the other to become the I-for-the-other and to internalise the perspective provided by the other. Being has to be understood as an event as it is bound by space and time, always once-occurrent by its very nature. One's being is an open-ended process. Bakhtin says that one's death is not part of one's life, as it does not happen in one's consciousness. For the other, one's being exists in space and time as a given. Bakhtin is concerned with the challenges in understanding being in its 'eventness'. 'Embodiment' is closely aligned with the idea of 'being' and 'event'. It is derived from the theology of Christianity which emphasises the principle of incarnation or embodiment. As a member of the Russian Orthodox Church, Bakhtin believed that the eventness of Christ's life as an embodied subject illustrates the resistance of being to abstract theoreticism.

Carnival: The medieval times in Europe found the emergence of carnival as a mode of defying the official culture of the times. The Catholic Church, the feudal system and the monarchy had absolute authority over society during this period. The only time common people could rise against the repressive apparatus of these regimes was during the time of the carnival. It afforded people the freedom to ridicule the priests, parody their sermons or hymns and question the unlimited freedom of the authoritarian state through acts and gestures which formed part of the public spectacle. These carnival forms gave rise to a large number of social discourses and public performances which became an essential part of the medieval society. After the medieval period, these forms entered literary discourses and found expression in the writings of authors such as Rabelais, Shakespeare and Voltaire.

Chronotope: Bakhtin uses the term 'chronotope' to indicate the spatial–temporal matrix that shapes a narrative text. Each genre has different chronotopes. It is through chronotopes that an author articulates the social life of a specific time and place. Chronotope is as much a cognitive construct as a narrative feature of texts. Chronotopes such as the road, unexpected encounters, castles or mansions, sudden recognition and the forest or hermitage signify an ideological world of echoes and suggestions that various genres put to use to shape an object of art. Bakhtin provided an exhaustive list of chronotopes based on the European novel.

Consciousness: Utterance is a sign of consciousness. Without utterance there can be no consciousness. Consciousness is always consciousness of a particular situation. Consciousness transforms the world as it addresses the world. It is an answering consciousness that participates in the process of transformation. A position of outsideness is central to achieve this answerability.

Dialogue: This is one of the keywords in Bakhtin's oeuvre. Every word enters into a dialogue or a dialogic relation with other words. Our words, thoughts and acts enter into dialogic relations with others' words, thoughts or acts to create meanings and values. Bakhtin feels that intertextual relations between words, texts and systems of thought weave a system of meanings for the entire society. Those words or texts which refuse to enter into such meaningful dialogic relations are monologic. A discourse which denies the dialogic nature of existence is monologic. For instance, epics are monologic as they speak on behalf of a hegemonic ideology that demands complete allegiance to their truth claims, just as authoritarian or repressive regimes stress that they have the last word on all matters.

Discourse: Discourse is the way in which language is used socially to convey shared meanings. Words that are in use constitute a discourse. The meanings of words are derived from the contexts of the discourses they are part of. Words are accented with the intentions and values of the speakers and the discourse always reflects those orientations. For Bakhtin, no sign is neutral. Discourses are understood differently by authors like Foucault. For Foucault, each subject gives rise to a discursive formation. For example, we can speak of colonial discourse or environmental discourse. Practices which constitute a subject result in a discourse.

Environment: I am constituted by my environment, which includes my situation as a whole. As an individual situated in a specific time and place, my circle of vision is determined by a specific location, my individual consciousness as the member of a social group and my acquired knowledge. Apart from these factors, my environment also includes elements that are accessible to me through the mediation of the other. The gift of the other is an important component of my environment.

Genre: Bakhtin speaks of speech genres which he divides into primary and secondary genres. In our everyday life, a number of situations recur and the language used on such occasions constitute a set of conventions which signify their meanings by the very nature of their generic forms. Among literary genres, Bakhtin talks of serious genres like the epic and tragedy, and serio-comic genres like Menippean satire and the Socratic dialogues. Talking about the weather and conversation across an enquiry counter are examples of primary speech genres. Apart from these primary speech genres, Bakhtin speaks of secondary speech genres which include literary genres like tragedy, epic and the novel. According to Bakhtin, the novel is the most complex modern literary genre. It resists canonisation. It also influences other genres, a process which Bakhtin terms 'novelisation' and describes at length. The novel can assimilate into its structure other genres such as poetry and drama, and even forms like letters and other forms of communication.

Heteroglossia: In the ancient period, contact between languages was rare. Each society or country had only one stable and unified language. As multinational societies emerged, 'polyglossia' (the cultural phenomenon of having two or more national languages) became common. During the Renaissance, as languages began to penetrate regions beyond that of their own origin, polyglossia became common. While polyglossia refers to 'multi-languagedness', heteroglossia implies the plurality of 'languages' within one language. Between the centripetal and centrifugal, or official and unofficial centres of power, a language displays different ideological orientations. It manifests different kinds of discourses which constitute the same national language. Heteroglossia has to be differentiated from 'polyphony', which refers to 'multi-voicedness'. This is a defining feature of Dostoevsky's novels, where the author and the hero confront each other on equal terms. For instance, the prevalence of Sanskrit, English, Tamil and Konkani along with Malayalam, in the state of Kerala may suggest heteroglossia, while different discourses within Malayalam are indicative of multiple ideological perspectives.

Ideology: For Bakhtin, any utterance is ideological. In that sense, the term 'ideology' refers to the way in which a given social group views the world. The English term 'ideology', as used by Marxist thinkers and their followers, implies a belief system that mediates the words or deeds of a subject in a society. A term like 'Ideological State Apparatus' makes it clear that institutions enforce the political ideology of the state apparatus through either coercion or consent. Bakhtin does not share this larger meaning of the term 'ideology'.

Meaning: Bakhtin does not hold the view that meaning is fixed and stable in time or space. He rejects the formalist and Marxist approaches to meaning, the former being text-bound and the latter being a product of extratextual factors. According to Bakhtin, meanings are always open-ended and they are produced through the dialogic relations between self and other, one and another and inside and outside. Since we are 'answerable', we have no choice but to address the world and be addressed by the world. Meaning results from the interaction between the addressor and the addressee. Bakhtin also distinguishes between the theme of an utterance, which refers to what is contextually unique to the utterance, and its meaning, which refers to those semantic or syntactic elements that are not context-specific.

The Novel: Bakhtin considers the novel as *the* literary genre of the modern period. He views it as a site of struggle between hegemonic worldviews and those opposed to them. The novel is a counter-narrative that contests canonised worldviews. The field of culture is characterised by a struggle between centrifugal and centripetal forces. While literary forms like the epic and tragedy may represent the 'official' views of a society, the novel contests such views. The novel evolved out of the carnivalised forms of literature which represented the popular domain of resistance. It is primarily 'heteroglottic' as it reflects the multiple languages of a society. It renders the word relative and fluid by denying sanctity to any particular utterance or worldview. While a form like the epic tends to look back into the past towards a fixed meaning, the novel speaks of becoming in open terms.

Outsidedness: I need the other to understand the world and complete myself. Similarly, the other needs me to know itself. That quality which is required of me to complete the other and complement the other's perception of his or her self is termed 'outsidedness'. I should go beyond the limits of my own self and enter the cognitive space of the other to achieve full self-knowledge. The author can give his hero the gift of self-perception because he is outside the hero.

Speech: Bakhtin discusses forms of speech in great detail. For him, it is important to distinguish between direct and reported speech. The accent or the voice of the speech or utterance decides its semantic orientation. 'Double-voiced speech', as it exists in novels and novelistic genres, has been discussed by Bakhtin in several contexts. The novelistic discourse tends to be double-voiced. Author–hero relations are reflected in the nature of novelistic speech patterns. Speech act theories put forward by Austin and Searle have further extended the domain of speech as conceived by Bakhtin.

Surplus of Vision: There is a limit to what I can see. The other sees me from a perspective and in a context in which I can never see myself. This is why Bakhtin says that the other, in relation to ourselves, has a 'surplus of vision' or an 'excess of seeing'. We will never be able to perceive in ourselves the given whole of our own personality. This surplus of seeing enables us to relate to the other and gain a better, more comprehensive view of ourselves.

Theoreticism: Bakhtin uses this term to indicate a content-based approach to knowledge and life. To think that content exhausts the significance or full value is to fall prey to 'theoreticism'. A scientific or legal statement may have a specific meaning within its own domain, but can be interpreted differently in another context. The ways of multiple interpretations in endless human contexts remain a distinct possibility for any concept or idea. Theoreticist thinking will always result in abstractions based on a fragmented understanding of its object. It will not be able to grasp the 'eventness' of an act or phenomenon, as it cannot give an account of its physicality and 'here-and-now-ness'. Bakhtin does not deny the scientific truth of an idea. For instance, the scientific explanation of the rainbow as a phenomenon does not exhaust the emotional response it gives rise to in the minds of millions of human beings. Bakhtin believes that knowledge of a general nature, like that of gravity, needs to be distinguished from knowledge or experience of a specific kind such as that about racism. In objectifying a once-occurrent event, we risk turning it into a theoretical event.

Utterance: An utterance can be as brief as a single sound like 'Ah' or an entire epic or novel. It is not purely a linguistic concept for Bakhtin. It is the locus of encounter between two self-consciousnesses, between mind and the world. An utterance comes into being in answer to another utterance and will, in turn, give rise to a chain of utterances. The word always demands to be heard and it becomes meaningful only when it is met with a response from the other.

Value/Evaluation: Bakhtin speaks of the 'social evaluation' of an utterance, by which he means those factors that make it socially and culturally specific. Social evaluation unites the material presence of the word with its meaning.

Voice: An utterance is always accented. Its voiced quality takes part in the construction of meaning. Voice reflects the values behind the consciousness that speaks. It has been pointed out that Russian words carry their own particular accents, much more than English words. Two words with the same spelling in Russian will have two meanings when they have different accents. When you listen to the other's voice, it is subjected to your intention and valuation and it is re-accented.

REFERENCES

Bakhtin, Mikhail M. *Art and Answerability: Early Philosophical Essays*. Ed. Michael Holquist and Vadim Liapunov. Trans. Vadim Liapunov. Austin: U of Texas P, 1990. Print.

---. *Speech Genres and Other Late Essays*. Trans. Vern W. McGee. Ed. Caryl Emerson and Michael Holquist. 1979. Austin: U of Texas P, 1986. Print.

---. *Toward a Philosophy of the Act*. Trans. Vadim Liapunov. Ed. Vadim Liapunov and Michael Holquist. Austin: U of Texas P, 1993. Print.

Suggested Reading

PRIMARY SOURCES

Bakhtin, Mikhail M. *Art and Answerability: Early Philosophical Essays*. Ed. Michael Holquist and Vadim Liapunov. Trans. Vadim Liapunov. Austin: U of Texas P, 1990. Print.

---. *Problems of Dostoevsky's Poetics.* Edited and translated by Caryl Emerson. Minneapolis: U of Minnesota P, 1984. Print.

---. *Rabelais and His World.* Trans. Hélène Iswolsky. 1968. Bloomington: Indiana UP, 1984. Print.

---. *Speech Genres and Other Late Essays*. Trans. Vern W. McGee. Ed. Caryl Emerson and Michael Holquist. 1979. Austin: U of Texas P, 1986. Print.

---. *The Dialogic Imagination: Four Essays*. Trans. Caryl Emerson and Michael Holquist. Ed. Michael Holquist. Austin: U of Texas P, 1981. Print.

Bakhtin M. M./Medvedev, P. N. *The Formal Method in Literary Scholarship: A Critical Introduction to Sociological Poetics.* Trans. Albert J. Wehrie. Baltimore: The Johns Hopkins UP, 1978. Print.

Voloshinov, V. N./Bakhtin, M. M. *Freudianism: A Critical Sketch.* Trans. I. R. Titunik. Ed. I. R. Titunik and Neal H. Bruss. Indianapolis: Indiana UP, 1987. Print.

---. *Marxism and the Philosophy of Language*. Trans. Ladislav Matejka and I. R. Titunik. Cambridge, MA: Harvard UP, 1986. Print.

Shukman, Ann, ed. *Bakhtin School Papers*. Somerton, Oxford: RPT Publications in association with Department of Literature, University of Essex, 1983. Print.

Morris, Pam, ed. *The Bakhtin Reader: Selected Writings of Bakhtin, Medvedev, Voloshinov.* London: Arnold Publishers, 1994. Print.

SELECT SECONDARY SOURCES

Bandlamudi, Lakshmi, and E. V. Ramakrishnan, eds. *Bakhtinian Explorations of Indian Culture: Pluralism, Dogma and Dialogue through History*. Singapore: Springer Nature, 2018. Print.

Brandist, Craig. *The Bakhtin Circle: Philosophy, Culture and Politics.* London and Sterling, VA: Pluto Press, 2002. Print.

Clark, Katerina, and Michael Holquist. *Mikhail Bakhtin.* Cambridge, MA: The Belknap Press (Harvard UP), 1984. Print.

Dentith, Simon, ed. *Bakhtinian Thought: An Introductory Reader.* London and New York: Routledge, 1996. Print.

Emerson, Caryl. *The First Hundred Years of Mikhail Bakhtin.* Princeton: Princeton UP, 1997. Print.

Gardiner, Michael. *The Dialogics of Critique: M. M. Bakhtin and the Theory of Ideology.* London: Routledge, 1993. Print.

Hirschkop, Ken. *Mikhail Bakhtin: An Aesthetic for Democracy.* New York and Oxford: Oxford UP, 1999. Print.

Hirschkop, Ken, and David Shepherd, eds. *Bakhtin and Cultural Theory.* Rev. ed. Manchester: Manchester UP, 2001. Print.

Holquist, Michael. *Dialogism: Bakhtin and His World.* London: Routledge, 1990. Print.

Kristeva, Julia. *Desire in Language: A Semiotic Approach to Literature and Art.* Ed. Leon S. Roudiez. Trans. Thomas Gora, Alice Jardine and Leon S. Roudiez. Oxford: Basil Blackwell, 1981. Print.

Lodge, David. *After Bakhtin: Essays on Fiction and Criticism.* London: Routledge, 1990. Print.

Mayerfeld Bell, Michael, and Michael Gardiner, eds. *Bakhtin and the Human Sciences: No Last Words.* Sage Publications Ltd., 1998. Print.

Morson, Gary Saul, and Caryl Emerson. *Mikhail Bakhtin: Creation of a Prosaics.* Stanford: Stanford UP, 1990. Print.

Morson, Gary Saul, and Caryl Emerson, eds. *Rethinking Bakhtin: Extensions and Challenges.* Evanston: Northwestern UP, 1989. Print.

Renfrew, Alastair. *Mikhail Bakhtin.* New York: Routledge, 2015. Print. Routledge Critical Thinkers.

———. *Towards a New Material Aesthetics: Bakhtin, Genre and the Fates of Literary Theory.* London: Legenda, 2006. Print.

Todorov, Tzvetan. *Mikhail Bakhtin: The Dialogical Principle.* Trans. Wlad Godzich. Minneapolis: U of Minnesota P, 1984. Print.

Other books in the series

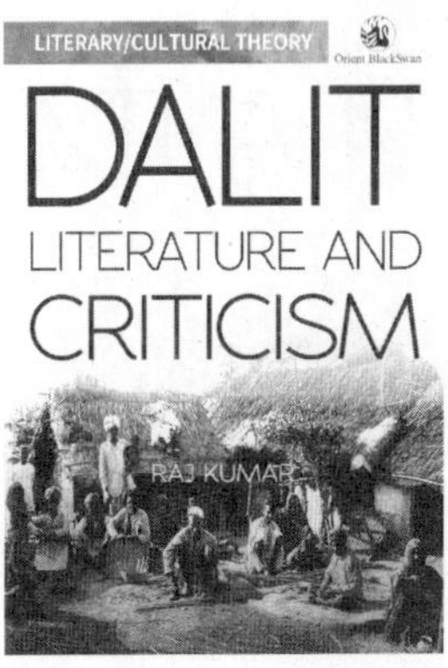

For more information, visit www.orientblackswan.com

Other books in the series

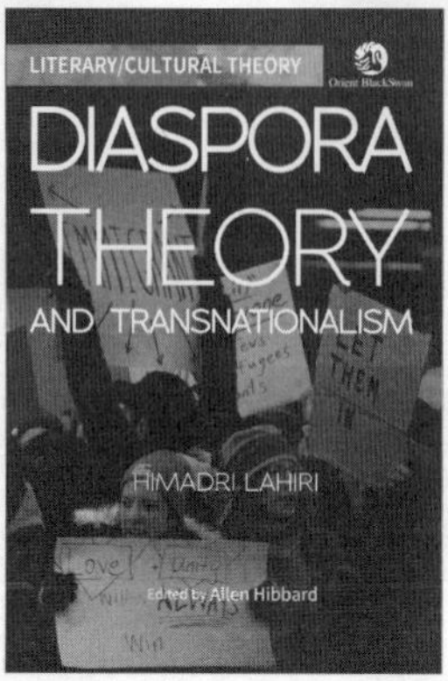

For more information, visit www.orientblackswan.com

Other books in the series

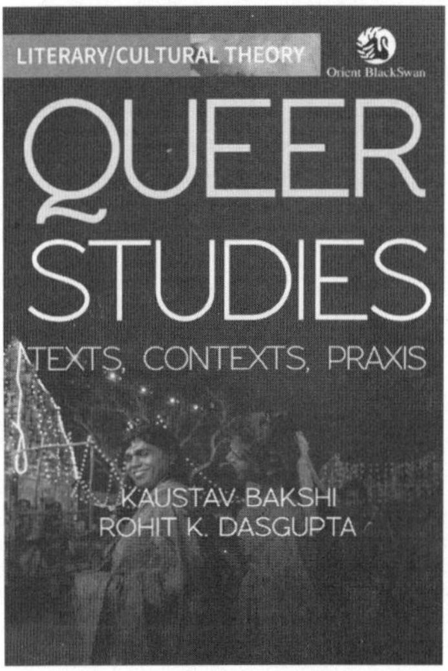

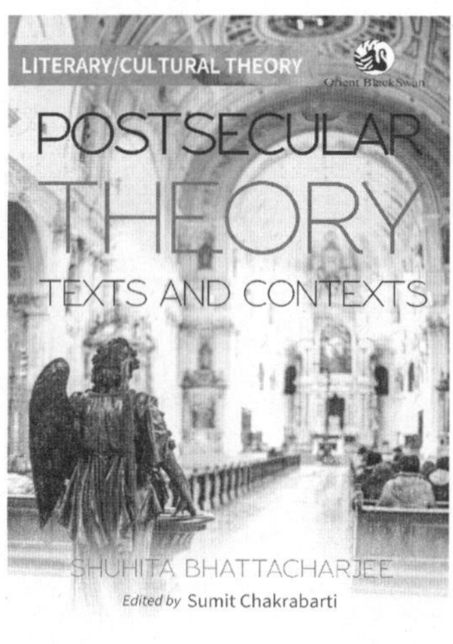

For more information, visit www.orientblackswan.com